THE DECKCHAIR GUIDE
TO BRIGHTON & HOVE

...by the people who live here...

QueenSpark Publishers
Brighton & Hove

Published by QueenSpark Publishers

Copyright QueenSpark Publishers 2007

QueenSpark is a non-profit community
publishing and writing organisation, which
for over thirty years has helped the people
of Brighton & Hove to tell their stories

QueenSpark Publishers,
49 Grand Parade, Brighton BN2 9QA.
Tel. 01273 571710.
www.queensparkbooks.org.uk,
www.thedeckchair.org.uk

The views and opinions expressed in
this guide do not necessarily reflect
the views of QueenSpark Publishers
or its current or former Directors

Copyright of photographs is acknowledged
where appropriate

ISBN 978-0-904733-28-0

A catalogue of this book is available at
the British Library

Reader Feedback
QueenSpark has made every effort to
credit all contributors to this publication
and to ensure that all the content is
accurate at the time of going to press,
but takes no responsibility for errors
and omissions herein. However we do
welcome any feedback or clarification
for inclusion in future reprints.
Write to us at 49 Grand Parade
or email us at: info@thedeckchair.org.uk

Editor: Tim Lay

Picture Editor: Helen Fitzgerald

Managing Editor: Sarah Hutchings

Design: Jon Wainwright at Alchemedia Design
www.alchemediadesign.com

Cover Design: Katie Davies and Amy Preston

Section writers: Glencora Bailey (Community),
James Burt (Free), Katy Evans (Drinking) and
Linda Verrall (Eating and Shops)

Additional Writing
John Riches & Sarah Hutchings

In addition to the writers, and hundreds of
local residents who completed Deckchair
questionnaires and lent their support, we would
particularly like to thank the following:

Claire Andrews
Kevin Bacon
Prue and Stanley Baker
Sebastian Coles
Rose Collis
Hilary Cooke
Sue Craig
Melita Dennett
Jennifer Drury
John Fisher
Grand Parade of Authors (GPoA)
Lucy Hermann
Jack Latimer
Vanora Leigh
Mikel Maron
Anne Morrison
MyBH interviewers group
Tom Sawyer and Siobhan Keaney at the
University of Brighton BA(Hons) Graphic Design

For permission to reproduce images:
Al Fresco, The Argus, Bali Brasserie, Blackout,
The Blanch House, Brighton & Hove
Neighbourhood Care Scheme, Brighton Peace
and Environment Centre, Will Eddy, David Gray,
Beatrice Haverich, Mischa Hewitt, Koba, The
Lavender Room, Henry Law, Shaun Oaten, Eman
Phillips, James Pike, Richard Rotter, The Royal
Pavilion and Museums, Brighton & Hove, The
Real Eating Company, Sevendials Restaurant,
Smash EDO, Peter Stocker of North Laine
Ceramics, Terre a Terre, Wagamama, JJ Waller
and the Whitehawk Community Food Project

A massive thanks to Jon Wainwright
at Alchemedia Design and Helen Fitzgerald
our picture editor

Maps: The maps at the back of the guide
are courtesy of www.openstreetmap.org
licensed by Creative Commons
Attribution-ShareAlike 2.0 license

This Guide was printed using vegetable based
inks and Elemental Chlorine Free paper, sourced
from Sustainable Forests

Contents

4   Introduction

10   Community

34   Eating

64   Drinking

84   Free Brighton & Hove

108   Shopping

138   Maps

152   Index

Welcome to The Deckchair Guide to Brighton & Hove

Hundreds of local people shared their knowledge and opinions in this guide book (see Deckchair Poll throughout) and many others volunteered their time to canvass local people, source images, and write about why they love this city (warts and all). What you won't find here are the latest trendy bars or the 'in' places to be seen - which are often beyond the financial reach of most people, and sometimes closed by the time they make it into print. Nor will you find a roll-call of chain shops and restaurants that can be found on any high street in the country - most of which are very visible to visitors anyway.

Brighton & Hove is a multi-faceted city and it is possibly its trendy, cosmopolitan side most people recognise. Local residents however are familiar with a much more fascinating, diverse place; and, like with good friends, this side takes longer to get to know. What is it really like to live here? Is it just 'London by the sea' as the media portrays? Or does it have its own unique identity?

For thirty-five years QueenSpark Books has been working with local people to tell the stories of this city and its people. The Deckchair Guide features excerpts from many of QueenSpark's out of print titles and old photographs which highlight how the place has changed. We hope that together they offer the reader a unique glimpse into the life of one of the UK's most dynamic and interesting cities.

About Town

Buses

Brighton & Hove Bus and Coach Company,

43 Conway Street, Hove
(01273) 886200 http://www.buses.co.uk
The city's bus service is very efficient, though some residents think fares are a bit pricey, particularly for short trips. Savers are currently £3.20 per day and there is a flat fare for a single trip of £1.70. **Top tip**: buying a pack of Saver tickets via the internet saves you money!

The Big Lemon,

8 Norfolk Street, Brighton
(01273) 327335
http://www.thebiglemon.com
The Big Lemon launched its first service in September 2007, the 42 / 42X, operating between Falmer Station and Brighton Station via Old Steine. Their buses run on locally-sourced used cooking oil in order to minimise their impact on the environment, and at £1 per journey or £2 the fares are competitive.

City Sightseeing,

www.city-sightseeing.com
Once you've bought your ticket (currently £6.50 Adults/ £2.50 Children) you can hop on and off the bus all day and it is valid for 24 hours. The whole tour takes 50 mins and there is an English Commentary throughout.

Taxis,

(01273) 205205/202020/822822/747474
The main taxi ranks in central Brighton are at the station and East Street. There is also one on Queen Square near the clocktower.

Tuc Tuc, (01273) 205000

www.tuctuc.co.uk
Email tuctuc@tuctuc.co.uk
The idea of running motorised rickshaws came to founder Dominic Ponniah when he was backpacking in Asia. At the time of publication the Brighton & Hove fleet was off the road for winter - check their website for more up-to-date information.

Brighton by bus

The West Pier on Brighton beach

Highlights

The beach – especially for barbecues in the evening or going for a swim in my lunchbreak when it's hot – then I can send gloating text messages to my mates who live in London. – Local resident

Playing golf on Hollingbury Hill – fantastic views! - Stella

The city has this fab creative vibe, which I love! – Helena

Checking out the graffiti in various places around town. A free-for-all art gallery with an exhibition that changes every week.
– Local resident

Its (the city's) do anything, live how you want ethos.
– Local resident

The North Laine. It seems to be the only place left where individuality hasn't sold out to multiples, big business or getting the tourists in! – Local resident

The Regency architecture reflects the growth of a fishing town into a fashionable resort. – Sarah

Montpelier Villas ... where the perfume of the lilac drifts over whitewash and the only sounds are birdsong and the crunch of cat-paw on gravel. Always worth a detour, especially if you include Clifton Terrace on route. – Local resident

The views at Ditchling Beacon are wonderful for clearing your head on summer evenings after work – the light is fantastic and the weather feels at its most intense – I have seen a triple rainbow there, which was an incredible sight.
– Local resident

It's a great place for doing yoga – loads of good teachers and some lovely studios.
– Local resident

Socialising and soaking up the sun. – Paul

Top Ten Buildings
(as voted in The Deckchair Poll)

1. The Royal Pavilion
Beautiful, different, iconic. – Jennifer
Even on the gloomiest day the Pavilion lifts my mood. – Rachel

2. Jubilee Library
Light, airy and easy to use. – Michael

3. Embassy Court
An example of art and architecture in its own right; but a David and Goliath story, of resilience against all opposition to save this icon. – Local resident

4. The West Pier
Skeletal West Pier looks cool, especially at sundown with starlings flying over it. – Local resident

5. The Dome

6. St Bartholomew's Church

7. St Peter's Church

8. Brighton Station
The glass roof – the Victorian splendour! – Tina

9. Duke of York's Cinema

10. Theatre Royal/St Peter's Church

The Pavilion

Brighton station

Top Ten Worst Things About The City

(as voted in The Deckchair Poll)

1. Rubbish/Litter
The streets and beach can get pretty grimy in the summer (people not taking their litter home/over flowing bins) which spoils the city for everyone. – Paula

2. Too expensive
It is a really expensive place to live yet wages are really low (in my experience). Rent, drinks, events all tend to be similarly priced to London yet we get no equivalent to London weighting. It makes it hard to enjoy all that Brighton has to offer when you can't afford to do anything!
– Local resident

What a load of rubbish

Cost of living – it's ridiculous, especially compared to wages – we're paying London prices with non-London salaries.
– Jennie

3. Traffic

4. Parking
I can no longer park outside my house as there are too many other cars, particularly if I return home after six thirty. – Vicky

5. Council planning
When I look back and remember what has been altered since the 1930s, someone once asked me who the greatest vandals were, I had no hesitation in answering: 'the town planning committee'.
– Local resident

6. (Tied) West Street/Seagulls
...they can get a bit aggressive and I'm always having to protect my lunch!
– Local resident

7. Crowds

8. Too Trendy

9. Homelessness

10. Chewing Gum everywhere

01

Brighton & Hove Community

Despite the attraction of its colourful and sometimes subversive vitality, Brighton & Hove is a British city like any other, and the problems here are as real as anywhere. Local reaction to these social and political problems tends to be very positive and many people across the city are using their skills, knowledge and energy to work towards change.

While the city's reputation as home to a left-leaning, socially aware, politically conscious population can sometimes feel a bit worn, on the whole it does seem true that if you want to change something, even if it's yourself, Brighton & Hove is one of the more inspiring places to try to do it.

This chapter features some of the groups, campaigns, organisations and projects that are unique to Brighton & Hove. It's not comprehensive but will give a flavour of some of the many socially/politically-focused groups the city has to offer. If you want to get involved, look no further….

Best Community Noticeboards

The noticeboard at Infinity Foods © David Gray www.imagesbrighton.com

Whether you're looking for a lift to Cornwall, a room to rent, or the nearest drumming class, these noticeboards should have the answer.

Arkwright's Deli (see page 119)
Situated in the front window

Bill's (see page 58)
Tucked away near the toilets

Hove Library (see page 98)
A community events board in the front hallway

Hove Station
A free noticeboard on platforms 1 & 2. Speak to Tim the 'Supreme Commander'

Infinity Foods (see page 116)
Situated in the front window

Taj (see page 118)
At the Taj on Western Road

SCIP List
SCIP or Sussex Community Internet Project is a fantastic online community notice board. More information about joining the SCIP List can be found at: www.scip.org.uk

Waterstone's
71 – 74 North Street, Brighton
(01273) 206017
In the fiction section on the first floor

Working For Change

Anarchist Teapot Mobile Kitchen

PO Box 74, BN1 4ZQ
www.eco-action.org/teapot
Anarchist Teapot was originally the
name of a string of cafes that squatted
in different locations around Brighton
from 1996 serving free tea and books.
In 1998 a group of volunteers
transformed it into a travelling kitchen,
supplying vegan, mostly organic (and
locally-sourced) GM-free food at low
cost for grassroots anarchist and
ecological gatherings including Earth
First, Animal Rights, Saving Iceland and
Radical Routes. They offer a selection of
variable menus and services, ranging
from stall snack-foods to large buffet
spreads and simple soup kitchens.

Bricycles

(01273) 552662
www.bricycles.org.uk
Bricycles is a voluntary campaigning and
social group for cyclists in Brighton and
Hove. It began in 1980 and quickly
gained a large membership. At the time,
there wasn't a single cycle rack or lane in
the city. Today Bricycles promotes cycling
as a healthy, fun form of transport and
represents cyclists' interests, organising
rides, social events and useful services
and meeting with the local council
weekly to express and discuss their views.

Brighton Animal Action

PO Box 307, BN2 1HW 07787 953 347
www.brightonanimalaction.org
Meet first and third Weds of the month,

© Brighton Peace and Environment Centre

7pm at the Cowley Club. Brighton
Animal Action coordinates various
campaigns to promote animal welfare in
the local area and give support to other
relevant national and global campaigns.
Fur, hunting, vivisection and live animal
exportation are all some of their other
major concerns.

Brighton Peace and Environment
Centre, 39 - 41 Surrey St, Brighton
(01273) 766610 www.bpec.org
Brighton Peace and Environment Centre
began 25 years ago as a small group

campaigning for nuclear disarmament. It has gradually expanded to become a Development Education Centre: working with the public to raise awareness and understanding of global problems. Facilities include a library, information and education resource centre with PC access and a meeting space for local groups. BPEC's interests span subjects surrounding social justice, peace, sustainable development and environmental protection.

Earthship Brighton Project
Stanmer Park, Lewes Road, Brighton
www.lowcarbon.co.uk
Tours – First and third Sunday of the month, meet 10:30am Stanmer Church on lawns in front of Stanmer House, £5. In 2000 Michael Reynolds gave a lecture to a Brighton audience about 'Earthships' and sustainable living. Following this, a number of people came together to form the Low Carbon Trust with the desire to build an Earthship in Brighton. At the same time Stanmer Organics expressed the need for a new community space. The two came together and the idea for the award-

winning Earthship Brighton project was born. Building began in 2003 and the city now has its first Earthship made predominantly from used tyres and run entirely on the planet's natural systems. Used year round as a community space and learning centre, Earthship Brighton is a place where people can come to see concrete examples of sustainable living in practice and discover more about the ways they might incorporate such examples into their own homes.

Green Women
Brighton Women's Centre 72 High Street, Brighton (01273) 503211
www.greenwomen.org.uk
Meetings monthly, every third Thursday Formed in 2006, this group is a focus point for women environmentalist activists who campaign for change, plan trips, hold talks and share ideas. Interests include women's health, alternative therapies, organic food and farming. Through educating themselves, bringing about personal lifestyle changes and forming networks, the Green Women make contributions towards a growing movement pushing for rapid environmental change.

Magpie Recycling Co-operative
Saunders Park Depot, Lewes Road, Brighton (01273) 684425
www.magpie.coop
What began 15 years ago as a kerbside collection scheme using converted milk-floats has now become a workers' co-operative, capable of collecting and recycling almost anything from cartridges to cooking oil and everything

Magpie Recycling © David Gray/www.imagesbrighton.com

As a UN Peace Messenger City, We Demand Brighton & Hove Pass A Resolution Condeming EDO MBM

Smash EDO take to the streets © Smash EDO

in between. Their services include domestic, commercial and office recycling collections, furniture removal and garden design. Magpie also runs *Shabitat*, the – cheap! – second-hand furniture, clothing and appliances warehouse on Lewes Road. They supply all re-housed homeless people in the area with furniture, and deliver - and demonstrate how to use - wormeries in schools.

Smash EDO

C/O Unemployed Centre,
6 Tilbury Place, Brighton 07891 405923
www.smashedo.org.uk
Meet every Wed, 4-6pm.
EDO MBM is a Brighton-based US arms multinational. Their products include bomb racks, release clips and arming mechanisms for warplanes. Smash EDO is an active group of local residents who have been noisily but nonviolently campaigning to shut down EDO through a combination of protest and awareness campaigning. More details of events and fundraising on the group's website.

Tubas Friendship and Solidarity

Group, 39-41 Surrey St 07984 438655
www.tubas.brightonpalestine.org
In April 2006 two Brighton residents visited Tubas in the Jordan Valley, Palestine. Troubled and shocked by what they encountered there, they returned to the UK to form the Brighton Tubas Friendship and Solidarity Group. The aim is to forge links between community organisations in Brighton and Tubas, to increase understanding of the realities of life for people in the occupied territories and support their struggle for civil and human rights. Their website archives reports and information from and about the Tubas region.

Join In

BASS
(Brighton Alliance of Sound Systems)

www.bass23.org
Run entirely by volunteers, BASS is a collective of people who use their knowledge and experience of sound systems to set up free, alternative and non-corporate parties. In 2001 all came together for the first ever event, a Solstice celebration and protest against the ban of free parties. Annual events include BASS on the beach every summer, and Community Fayre on The Level every autumn.

Baby Boogie

At 10 libraries across Brighton & Hove (01273) 296960
www.citylibraries.info/children/babyboogie.asp
Part of a campaign to encourage more families to become library users, Baby Boogie is a musical rhyme time class for pre-school children and their parents or carers. For half an hour kids can play instruments, dance, sing songs and chant rhymes to their heart's content. Nora, who organises the increasingly popular sessions, now holds them in 10 different libraries across Brighton & Hove. After the sessions health visitors

© Brighton & Hove Neighbourhood Care Scheme

offer information and advice. It has developed into a valuable social, support and advice network for parents and carers. Instruments are available to borrow from Whitehawk library. Various libraries participate and sessions are free. See website or flyers in libraries for more details.

Brighton & Hove Neighbourhood Care Scheme, 1st Floor Intergen House 65 – 67 Western Road, Hove
(01273) 775888 www.ncs.bhci.org
This project connects people to their neighbourhoods by matching them with volunteers who support them in simple ways, such as helping with odd jobs, doing gardening or just visiting them.

More information on becoming a volunteer is available on the website.

Brighton Bothways
www.myspace.com/brightonbothways
07867 741025
Weekly social, 8pm at **The Black Lion**, 14 Black Lion St, Brighton
A group for bisexuals who live, work or socialise in the city, Brighton Bothways welcomes people of all ages, gender, backgrounds and interests to join them in various social activities. Although primarily for bisexual people, they welcome friends and family of bi-people as well as the bi-friendly, open-minded and non-judgemental. Interested in creating a liberated space for bisexuals

who feel isolated from both mainstream heterosexual and lesbian and gay culture, they put on all kinds of things from workshops to book groups and film nights. For Winter Pride they speed dated, foam wrestled and swam naked in the sea and in the summer they organise an annual camping event.

Brighton History Centre

Brighton Museum and Art Gallery, Pavilion Gardens, Brighton
(01273) 296972
www.citylibraries.info/localhistory
If you are interested in local history, make sure you visit Brighton History Centre which you'll find upstairs at Brighton Museum and Art Gallery. The centre holds an extensive range of material belonging to Brighton & Hove City Council and has staff on hand to help you use the resources and facilities.

Brighton Ourstory

PO Box 2861, BN1 IUN
www.brightonourstory.co.uk
Brighton Ourstory collects and preserves lesbian and gay history, with a special focus on Brighton & Hove. Ourstory's main interest is in the ordinary lives of gay and lesbian people. Working as an oral history group, they record testimonies and gather materials to capture impressions of lives and reproduce them in different forms, from exhibitions and publications to performances (such as the Bona Books exhibition at the Jubilee library).

Brighton Women's Centre

72 High Street, Brighton
(01273) 698036
www.womenscentre.org.uk
Drop-in Mon, Wed, Thurs 9:30am– 2.30pm, Tues 5-7pm.
Brighton Women's Centre is based in bright premises in the heart of Kemp Town. It offers a comprehensive range of social services: low-cost professional counselling, a women-only drop-in service offering support, complementary therapy, advice and information, Ofsted registered day care facility, library, and free PC and internet access. The drop-in lounge and conference rooms also act as meeting space for other Brighton-based women's groups and community events. Run by women for women, the centre aims to provide support for women of all backgrounds, enabling them to lead more fulfilling, creative and independent lives.

Manager of the Women's Centre Mary Baldock answers a couple of questions…

Could you tell us a little bit about the Brighton Women's Centre's past?
Brighton Women's Centre was set up in 1974 by a collective of women determined to offer a safe space for women to find support and overcome social isolation. By 1991 it had become a registered charity. Through the determination of its extremely dedicated volunteers it has now been in existence for 33 years. In that time it has incubated new ideas which have spun-off into

© CEDP

independent projects (Oasis and Refuge), and provided a nurturing base for many groups and ideas: mental and physical support services, information and advice, training courses to foster self esteem, and arts and entertainment projects.

Tell us about your new premises and future plans.

Recently housed in a new building by a generous benefactor the BWC is now enjoying a new vibrancy and importance as a community resource. We are currently redeveloping the building to increase our space for counselling and therapies. We are consulting with other local agencies and our service users with the aim of further developing services to meet the needs of women in Brighton, Hove and surrounding areas.

Chinese Centre

113 Queens Road, Brighton
(01273) 234800
www.cedp.org.uk Open Mon-Sat,
Drop-in Mon, Wed, Fri, Sat, 2-6pm.
The Chinese community in Brighton includes people from Hong Kong, Macao, Singapore, Taiwan and Malaysia. The Chinese Centre aims to help Chinese people of all backgrounds, whether new migrants and students or those born in Britain. Specifically they organise cultural awareness training, events and activities and provide information about educational opportunities. They currently run a voluntary English language teaching programme in China. Every month they throw parties, with karaoke and Chinese food. People can learn Mandarin, join calligraphy and

© The Circus Project

have put on a number of productions over the years, independently and with the Streets of Brighton Festival.

City Synergy

Ridgeland House, 165 Dyke Road, Hove
(01273) 697339/730906
www.citysynergy.co.uk
City Synergy was formed in 2002 as an offshoot of Leisure Link, with the aim of providing social and sports activities in the evenings and weekends to people with vision impairment. Regular activities include walks, tenpin bowling, theatre visits, trips, social gatherings and tandem bicycle riding. City Synergy is also planning to offer arts workshops for the visually impaired in conjunction with local learning difficulties charity, Spiral. City Synergy aims to present a positive image of vision impairment and disability in general and they're always looking for new members and volunteers.

traditional painting workshops or find out more about the significance of symbolism in Chinese culture and why it is that people dance around like dragons with drums during festivals.

The Circus Project

Hangleton Community Centre, Hove
(01273) 884732
www.thecircusproject.co.uk
In the 1990s husband and wife Dave and Emma Taylor, both trained trapeze artists, moved to Brighton and needed somewhere to train. They set up The Circus Project in 1999, which provides lots of different services as well as reliable practice and performance space. They also hold workshops and training programmes for the young and old and

The Clare Project

Community Base, 113 Queen's Road, Brighton www.clareproject.org.uk
Mon–Fri 7–9pm. Helpline: 07776 232100
For the past six years the Clare Project has been offering a safe and confidential space for people who want to talk about subjects surrounding gender identity. The organisation provides support, as well as information and also gets together for monthly meals, swimming sessions and other occasional events. Drop-in sessions are on Tuesdays 2:30-5:30pm at Dorset Gardens Methodist Church, Dorset Gardens (near St. James's Street), Brighton.

The Grand Parade of Authors

The **Grand Parade of Authors** (GPoA) is a group of homeless writers who meet weekly to share their work and inspire each other to write creatively. A lot of their work can be seen on the Deckchair website www.thedeckchair.org.uk

Journalist Vanora Leigh interviews four members of GPoA...

Brighton is an expensive city, even for those with good incomes. So what's it like if you have nowhere to live and pennies rather than pounds in your pocket?

Chris, who spent four and a half months living in the Churchill Square car park in 2006, is adamant that whatever the hardships he'd rather be in Brighton, his home town, than any other place.

It's the diversity of Brighton that appeals, he says. It's more like a dozen different villages than a city. I've worked in London and there are some great people there but in Brighton people are willing to open up and talk to you whereas there's a sort of reluctance to do that in other parts of the country.

Chris, 47, lost his job as a bar manager in the winter of 2005 and found himself without a roof over his head. His salvation was the Jubilee Library.

When I was on the streets it was the only warm place I knew, he says. I didn't know about First Base for the homeless then.

He also spent hours in the city's Museum and Art Gallery enjoying the free exhibitions. Now living in a hostel, Chris is currently working on a book with other writers who have experienced homelessness. He's also had four articles published in *The Big Issue* in 2006.

Simon, 41, is proud to be a Brightonian. In the past he's been to prison several times but has always returned to the city, even though it's often meant sleeping rough.

What I really enjoy is walking through The Lanes at night when all the lights are on – it's magical!

Neither **Steve** or '**B**' were born in Brighton but came here, liked what they saw and stayed. Steve, 49, has had a series of good, well paid jobs in banking, IT and journalism. He's also an alcoholic.

I first came to Brighton with my then partner for a friend's wedding, he says. We both thought this was exactly the sort of place we wanted to be.

So they moved from London to Brighton but things went badly wrong and the relationship broke down.

Now I'm on housing benefits, says Steve. I've never slept rough but I've gone from having it all to having nothing. Since moving here everything seems to have gone wrong – but that's not Brighton's fault. I still like the city's energy and I love the beach. The downside? Well it is a bit youth orientated.

When Londoner 'B',31, arrived in Brighton he thought it was a great place and decided to stay for six months. That was 12 years ago. In those 12 years he has lived in squats, on people's floors and on the streets. Now he lives in a small rented flat, and has written his first book.

London was making me sick, it was so grey, he says. Brighton is just the opposite. I stay here because there's so much going on – I love the parks, I love the people. It's simply a great place.

East Brighton Bygones

39 Manor Hill, Brighton (01273) 687700
www.bygones.org.uk
Founded in 2003, this discussion group
for local people with an interest in the
history of life in East Brighton meets at
2pm, on the second Wednesday of the
month at Valley Social Centre,
Whitehawk Way, Brighton. Visit the
group's website for more information.

Homeless and Lonely Organisation
at St Anne's (HALO)

Fitzherbert Centre, Upper Bedford
Street, Brighton (01273) 602824
Mon - Fri, 10-1pm.
Originally founded and run by the nuns
of St. Anne's, this day centre (one of a
number in the city) provides immediate
advice and support. They're open every
day from 10am serving tea, coffee and
toast, with lunches for 20p at noon. They
have two shower facilities and people
can take away clothing on Mondays,
Tuesdays and Wednesdays.

Migrant English Project

Cowley Club, 12 London Rd, Brighton
www.migrantenglishproject.org
Monday 1-4pm.
Following an inspiring trip to a No
Borders camp in Germany (a group that
supports free migration and works to
abolish borders and resist deportations),
Brighton's Migrant English Project was
set up by a group of local teachers who
wanted to provide useful services and
resources for refugees and enable them
to connect with new communities. The
weekly drop-in session at the Cowley
Club offers free English lessons for
asylum seekers and refugees as well as
general information, support and advice.
Children are welcome.

Mosaic: Black and Mixed Parentage
Family Group

Community Base, 113 Queen's Road,
Brighton (01273) 234017
www.mosaicbrighton.org.uk
Mosaic is a large community organisation
of Black, minority ethnic and mixed
parentage families and individuals with
a diverse and continually growing
membership. They work to create safe,
supportive, anti-racist, culturally diverse
environments for members and to
represent their interests. Projects, services
and activities include drop-in social
gatherings and excursions, a wide-
reaching detailed community newsletter,
weekly playgroup, library, resource centre
and helpline.

Moulsecoomb Forest Garden
and Wildlife Project

Behind Moulsecoomb railway station.
(01273) 707656
The Moulsecoomb Project combines
seven different plots, each dedicated to
different types of gardening activity -
from organic and forest to wildlife and
even 'outlawed' vegetable gardening
(cultivating rarities like the broad ripple
yellow currant tomato). Much of their
work is with young people from local
schools, educating kids about
conservation and growing. The project is
open to all who are interested, regardless
of experience. Some areas of the
allotment are left alone for wildlife, or
uncultivated for gardeners to picnic,

The Sudanese Coptic Association © Eman Phillips

sunbathe or bake potatoes under the fire. New foods that might be useful in the future are cultivated and endangered plants from the past are protected.

My Brighton and Hove
www.mybrightonandhove.org.uk
This award-winning website with over 8,000 pages of living history about Brighton and Hove actively encourages people to share their memories and photos of the city. It is a collective pooling of information, knowledge and opinions about Brighton and Hove - as it is today and as it was in the past.

Queer Mutiny Brighton
Cowley Club, 12 London Road.
queermutinybrighton@riseup.net
Queer Mutiny Brighton are a loose bunch of radical queers of all sexualities who meet regularly in Brighton to talk to each other, socialise and get active. A DIY collective, the group is what people want it to be, whether that takes the form of talks, workshops, parties, meetings or action. All are committed to fighting prejudice, linking up with other campaigns, learning from each other, creating alternatives and celebrating queer identity. They say they aim to politicise a commercial queer population and queerify a sexist radical community.

The Sudanese Coptic Assoc.
Southwick Leisure Centre.
www.sudanesecoptic.com
Dr. Sobhi Yagoub 07775 630143
Meet every other Sunday between 4-10pm.

The Whitehawk Community Food Project

**The Whitehawk Community
Food Project**
Whitehawk Hill, East Brighton
www.thefoodproject.org.uk
07751 076395/07900 126817
Thurs/Sun, 12 til dusk.
At the top of Whitehawk Hill Road,
behind the Brighton Racecourse, and
through the warren-like maze of
allotments, you'll eventually come to a
stretch of tall woven wooden fencing
which marks the Whitehawk Community
Food Project. Here you can rest and peer
down over row upon row of worn-out
looking housing and further beyond, the
sea, deceptively calm from here,
sweeping out as far as it's possible to see.

The allotment site is one of the more
established in the city with a lot of
people working on the well-kept and
abundant gardens. This patch of land
was disused until John and Jacob (who
had only been gardening for six months)
and a couple of others decided to take it
over in 2000. Since then, the plot has
been totally transformed, and now
works as a productive garden with fruit,

vegetable and herb beds, polytunnels,
ponds, an orchard area, hens and one
big noisy cockerel.

They hold weekly school classes
teaching kids about different fruits and
vegetables, how to grow and how to
build. The classes have excellent word of
mouth and been gaining popularity over
time. Kids can get involved in any number
of tasks – building ponds, planting crops,
digging beds, feeding hens, trying out the
food that is grown there.

The Food Project uses organic,
biodynamic and permaculture
techniques, which in I-don't-know-how-
to-grow-a-tomato speak means
absolutely everything is pesticide free,
left to find and follow its own natural
balanced course. Things sprout
depending on the time of year, the main
period of growth being around June,
although John points out that he's
noticed significant changes over recent
years with crops, trees and flowers all
sprouting earlier each spring: concrete
signs of global warming.

On Thursdays, Sundays and holidays
throughout the year they open the site
to the public; all are invited to come
along and help out for as long as they
want in return for fresh seasonal produce.
No gardening experience is necessary,
just an interest in learning how.

Whitehawk Community Food Project
really is a hidden little haven. With the
stunning views of the city, the calm air
and friendly company, this place is living
proof that the heart of a community
doesn't always have to be at its centre.

The Project's polytunnels, overlooking Brighton

Learning about new foods at the Project

In 1990 there were only a few Sudanese families in Brighton but, every Saturday, in private flats, they held a Coptic Orthodox mass. These were conducted by a priest who travelled down from Croydon each weekend. (The Faith Project – QueenSpark Books 2006).

The political and religious consequences of the 1989 military coup in the Sudan resulted in a mass exodus of many Sudanese people to Britain, Canada and the United States during the subsequent years. Brighton now has a relatively large Sudanese population (between 5,000 and 6,000 people), many of whom have come here as refugees. The Coptic Association was formed in 1992 to meet their needs. Currently, services include informal support among members, individual advice and advocacy to support members in their dealings with official bodies and other voluntary agencies, an Arabic language school for children, and outings and social events throughout the year.

RareKind

104 Trafalgar Street, Brighton
(01273) 818170
www.rarekind.co.uk
RareKind are a collective of Brighton/London-based artists interested in graffiti and hip hop orientated urban art. Independent artists in their own right, RareKind have also been at the centre of activities moving the scene forward and representing it in the public domain. There's a gallery in the North Laine, displaying free-hand spray painted canvases, screen printed and hand painted clothing. They stock a wide range of US and UK hip hop on vinyl and CD, as well as books, magazines and DVDs and hold monthly open mic/deck nights. They also run the 'CanControl' scheme in conjunction with councils, schools and youth workers across the South East, organising graffiti art sessions for kids.

Writing Organisations

Brighton Nightwriters

(01273) 505642
www.nightwriters.org.uk
A group of writers who meet weekly to discuss and read their work aloud. 7.30pm every Wednesday upstairs at the Pub With No Name, 58 Southover Street, Brighton. See website for more details.

New Writing South

9 Jew Street, Brighton (01273) 735353
www.newwritingsouth.com
With playwright and former arts consultant Chris Taylor at the helm, New Writing South (NWS) is a vibrant organisation at the heart of the creative community. Open to all new writers, and organisations wishing to work with writers, NWS aims to identify and nurture talent, encourage creativity and offer resources to all creative writers in the South East region. See website for more information.

QueenSpark Books

49 Grand Parade, Brighton
(01273) 571710
www.queensparkbooks.org.uk
www.thedeckchair.org.uk

The city's only non-profit community publishing organisation, QueenSpark publishes books about local people's lives and also runs a variety of projects around writing, publishing and local history. See websites for more information.

The South

49 Grand Parade, Brighton
(01273) 571700
www.thesouth.org.uk
The South is a writers' network and literary arts agency offering a range of services for writers. This includes professional development, writing workshops and event hosting. See website for more details.

Sussex Playwrights

New Venture Theatre, Bedford Place, Brighton www.sussexplaywrights.com
Monthly Sunday meetings, 7pm.
Sussex Playwrights has been running for over 70 years. Founded by Charles Walker in 1935, Constance Cox, Philip King and Judy Upton are just a few of the successful playwrights who have been members at one time or another. Budding and published playwrights get together and objectively consider each others work (there are also actors' readings). Sometimes conversations have led to productions, such as one that was performed at the Annual National Playwrighting competition, but primarily the group is about providing discussion and support for fellow writers. The group is also open to theatre buffs who don't write.

Web Communities

Active for Life
www.activeforlife.org.uk
Details local sports + activities groups, classes and sessions.

Argus Forum
http://forum.theargus.co.uk
General forum for discussion.

Brighton Activist
www.brightonactivist.net
Resource site for activism and events in Brighton.

Brighton and Hove Community and Voluntary Sector Forum
www.cvsectorforum.org.uk
Community and voluntary organisations forum.

B+H Issues Forum
http://forums.edemocracy.org/groups/bh
Web/email forum for discussing Brighton and Hove issues.

Brighton Irish Arts Network
www.sureitsirish.com
Irish arts and culture site for Brighton and Sussex.

Brighton New Media
www.brightonnewmedia.org
"Email discussion list for the local new media community".

Community Brighton
www.community.brighton.co.uk
Info/resource site for community/voluntary groups.

E. Sussex Community Info Service
www.escis.org.uk
Database of local and community information.

© David Gray www.imagesbrighton.com

Green Brighton
www.greenbrighton.com
Add-your-own map of green places
in Brighton.
Linux User Group
www.brighton.lug.org.uk
Brighton Linux user group.
My Brighton and Hove
www.mybrightonandhove.org.uk
(See above).
Radio Reverb 97.2 FM
www.radioreverb.com
Brighton and Hove's community
radio station.
Rough Music
www.roughmusic.org.uk
"Brighton's trouble makin' dirt diggin'
monthly".
SchNEWS
www.schnews.org.uk
Prominent wide-reaching radical
news sheet.

Southcoast Indymedia
www.southcoast.indymedia.org.uk
Independent open news site covering
the Sussex area.
Real Brighton www.realbrighton.co.uk
Listings for gay related things in
Brighton.
University of Sussex Students' Union
www.ussu.info
Info site for students.
University of Brighton Students' Union
www.ubsu.net
Info site for students.

Listings

Recreation

King Alfred Leisure Centre
Kingsway, Hove, (01273) 290290
Prince Regent Leisure Centre
North Road, Brighton, 0844 999 6236
Stanley Deason Leisure Centre
Wilson Ave, Brighton, (01273) 694281
Withdean Leisure Centre
Tongdean Lane, Withdean,
(01273) 542100

Community Centres

**Brighthelm Church
and Community Centre**
North Road, Brighton, (01273) 821512
Carden Park Community Centre
Carden Hill, Brighton (01273) 540779
Cornerstone Community Centre
Church Road, Hove (01273) 327757
Fitzherbert Community Centre
Upper Bedford Street, Brighton,
(01273) 602824
Fresh Start Community Centre
131 Lewes Road, Brighton,
(01273) 621267
Friends Meeting House
Ship Street, Brighton, (01273) 770258
Hangleton Community Centre
Harmsworth Crescent, Hove,
(01273) 292962
Hanover Community Centre
33 Southover Street, Brighton,
(01273) 694873
Hollingdean Community Centre
Thompson Road, Brighton,
(01273) 236160

Kemp Town Crypt Community Centre
St. Georges Road (01273) 888444
Meadowview Community Centre
Meadowview, Brighton (01273) 687563
Moulsecoomb Community Centre
Moulsecoomb Way, Brighton,
(01273) 622206
Patcham Community Centre
Ladies Mile Road, Brighton
(01273) 508376
Phoenix Community Centre
2 Phoenix Place, Brighton
(01273) 621794
Preston Park Centre
18 Preston Park Avenue, Brighton
(01273) 565049
West Hill Hall
Compton Avenue, (01273) 327976
**Whitehawk Youth
and Community Centre**,
Whitehawk Road, Brighton,
(01273) 293636
Woodingdean Community Centre
Warren Road, (01273) 685940
Young People's Centre
69 Ship Street, (01273) 887886

Useful Addresses

**Brighton and Hove Disability
Advice Centre**
6 Hove Manor, Brighton, (01273) 203016
Brighton and Hove Jewish Centre
81 Denmark Villas, Hove, (01273) 295956
**Brighton and Hove TUC
Unemployed Workers' Centre**
Frank Elvy House, 4 Crestway Parade,
Brighton, (01273) 540717
Brighton Youth Centre
64 Edward Street, Brighton,
(01273) 681368

Community Base
113 Queens's Road, Brighton,
(01273) 234002
Community Mental Health Centre
76-9 Buckingham Road, Brighton,
(01273) 749500
Cowley Club
(Radical Left collectively run community
space), London Road, Brighton,
(01273) 696104
First Base Day Centre
St Stephen's Hall, Montpelier Place,
Brighton, (01273) 326844
Impact Initiatives
(social inclusion for the young and old),
Brighthelm, North Road, Brighton,
(01273) 821914
Kaye Day Centre
88 Sackville Road, Hove, (01273) 295956
Phoenix Arts Association
10-14 Waterloo Place, Brighton,
(01273) 603700
Polish Centre
Polski Dom, 78 Farm Road,
(01273) 205864
Resource Centre
6 Prior House, Tilbury Place, Brighton,
(01273) 671213
Somerset Day Centre
62 St. James's Street, (01273) 699000
Spectrum LGBT Community Forum
6 Bartholomews, Brighton,
(01273) 723123
St Patrick's Trust
3 Cambridge Road, Hove (01273) 733151

**The Basement, Arts Production
South East**
(visual, performing, live arts resource
and support centre) Ground Floor,
Argus Lofts, Kensington Street
(01273) 699733
**The Bridge Community
Education Centre**
Lucraft Road, Brighton (01273) 294929
**Threshold Women's Mental
Health Initiative**
14 St. Georges Place, Brighton
(01273) 622886
Tower House Day Centre
Tower Gate, London Road, Brighton
(01273) 296330
Valley Social Centre
Whitehawk Way (01273) 673792
**Brighton Lesbian
and Gay Switchboard**
(01273) 204050
Rape and Crisis Centre
(01273) 203773
Women's Refuge Project
(01273) 622822

02

Eating in Brighton & Hove

Some of the city's best restaurants are very much tucked-away, off the tourist track and not at all obvious as you walk around. There are restaurants here the like of which you won't find anywhere else. Barry at the Tureen is one and Prompt Corner is another - both have been around for many years. So for a true taste of this city, get yourself a street map, avoid the big chain eateries and hunt these gems down.

Price categories are a rough indication of how much you can expect to pay for two courses whilst sharing a bottle of wine. All information correct at the time of writing.

Happy eating.

Carluccio's © Shaun Oaten

The City's Top Ten Restaurants

(as voted in The Deckchair Poll)

(**£**) Cheap – under £20 per head
(**££**) Reasonable – under £30 per head
(**£££**) Expensive – over £30 per head

1. Terre a Terre, 71 East Street,
Brighton (01273) 729051 (**£££**)
www.terreaterre.co.uk

Really imaginative veggie food. Their Terre a Tapas has a selection of lovely things from the menu and is perfect for people who can't choose what to have. (And it's also big enough to share!) – Local resident.

Terre à Terre is a well-known Brighton vegetarian restaurant with an extensive menu (its home-made condiments - sauces, pickles and dressings - are for sale, both at the restaurant and online); house specialities include the Terre à Tapas and Santa Rini Linguine. There is a kid's menu and high chairs and there

are discounts for members of the Vegetarian Society. Closed on Mondays.

2. Due South, 139 King's Road Arches, Brighton (01273) 821218 (**£££**)
www.duesouth.co.uk

Fantastic locally sourced organic food, no fuss, good service and brilliant sea views – Local resident

The location and architecture of this place would be reason enough to go. It's in the Arches directly opposite the beach. Upstairs there is a large half-moon window, where you can sit with your shellfish and watch the sea. The majority of the ingredients come from within a 35-mile radius - local fish, wild mushrooms, free range lamb, local beer, to name but a few – and as the menu makes the best of seasonal produce,

© Terre a Terre

Due South © Will Eddy

Carluccio's © Henry Law

it frequently changes. Observer Food Monthly voted it Best Seaside Restaurant in Britain and it has won an AA rosette two years in a row, so say no more! Also of note is that this is the only venue on the beachfront that is licensed for marriages and civil partnerships.

3. Carluccio's, Jubilee St, Brighton (01273) 690493 (£££)

We have included this as Deckchair pollsters voted it their third favourite restaurant in the city, but with over thirty four sites across England this chain certainly doesn't need any help from us. It's easy to see why it's so popular: they serve excellent coffee, the décor is clean and contemporary and the dishes are usually of a high standard. If recent articles in the press are to be believed,

the staff at this chain are on very low wages. Seeing as Mr Carluccio's doing so well, perhaps he could think about paying them a bit more?

4. Al Fresco, King's Road Arches, Brighton (01273) 206523 (££)
www.alfresco-brighton.co.uk

The design of this glass rotunda is truly amazing - an Art Deco-style Italian restaurant flooded with natural light, with seamless 360 degree views. It fits in well with the other Art Deco buildings on the seafront and the owners have kept the outside looking the same as it has always been. One tick for preservation! It's not the best value in town but the sea views and the fishbowl experience make it worth a visit. À la carte choices include the linguine al'aragosta (linguine

© Al Fresco

with half a fresh lobster, crayfish tails and rich tomato sauce), and filetto ai porcini. There are disabled facilities and a changing room for babies.

5. Planet India, 54 Preston Street, Brighton (01273) 275717 (£)

It could've been invented for me and, like quite a lot of other devotees, I feel as if I own shares in the whole venture, even if my dividend comes in the form of tarka dhal rather than a cheque. – Ian

This place is more of an Indian bistro than anything else - it looks just like a café but serves restaurant-level food – and is very popular with those 'in the know'. All the usual curries, snacks, side orders and a few different items such as tarka dall curry (chana lentils cooked with garlic and ginger). Until recently it was completely veggie, but now serves ethically sourced chicken and lamb. Unusually for an Indian bistro there is Lithuanian beer, Polish lager, Swedish pear cider, vegan wine and luxury Polish potato vodka. And why not? Closed Mondays. *At the time of writing the owner told us they might be moving, but they will keep the same telephone number.*

6. The Gingerman, 21a Norfolk Square, Brighton (01273) 326688 (£££)
www.gingermanrestaurants.com
The Gingerman has a sister restaurant at Drakes Hotel, Marine Parade and a newly opened pub, The Ginger Pig in Hove Street (see page 78 in the Drinking section). Small and tucked away it is

© Wagamama

perfect for intimate dates or confidante lunches with your *bestest* friend. Neutral, minimalist décor, wooden floor, white linen, brown leather sofas and wooden chairs together with candles on the tables create a calming space. Starters include a twist of tradition such as roast beef on dripping toast and mains include roasted partridge with fondant potato, and loin of venison. There is no children's menu but children's portions can be provided. There are baby-changing facilities and the restaurant is suitable for disabled guests.

7. Kambi's, 107 Western Rd, Brighton (01273) 327934 **(£)**

Kambi's is a kebab shop on the outside and a Lebanese restaurant inside. It is run by a friendly family and they serve delicious mezze – Local resident

A Lebanese restaurant that also serves Iranian and Arabic food. Two-thirds of the menu is vegetarian and many dishes are suitable for vegans. This restaurant was included in a national round-up of the top 40 budget eateries in The Guardian and has also won other awards. There is a very quick takeaway counter at the front of the restaurant. The atmosphere is suitably Middle Eastern with music redolent of ancient cities and dusty bazaars. The food consists of hot and cold mezze and specialities include batinjan, machbous and jewji. Traditional desserts, juices and smoothies round the menu off nicely. No children's facilities.

8. Wagamama, The Argus Building, 30 Kensington St, off North Road, Brighton (01273) 688892 **(£)**

It's easy to see why this extremely popular noodle bar chain made it into the Deckchair Top Ten. Set out like a stylish canteen, the bench seating and long tables encourage interaction between diners and the simple no frills service is efficient and friendly. Oh and did we mention they serve free green tea?

9. Pintxo People, 95 Western Road, Brighton (01273) 732323 **(££)**
www.pintxopeople.co.uk

The wonderfully-named Pintxo People (pronounced 'pin-cho') is a Basque and Catalan tapas bar and restaurant. Upstairs is a full-blown impressive modern restaurant serving tapas with a twist, such as octopus with broken potatoes and chorizo. The quality of the food is reflected in its AA rosette award. Downstairs is more traditional and serves small pintxo dishes for a £1 a shot. The desserts are to die for and drinks include Spanish cider. There are baby-changing facilities and facilities for the disabled.

10. Moshi Moshi, Bartholomew's Square, Brighton (01273) 719195 **(££)**
www.moshimoshi.co.uk

This Japanese restaurant claims to be the first conveyor belt-style restaurant in Britain. It pays to be a member here as, if you are, every Sunday the sushi dishes are just £1.90 and you get a free meal on your birthday as well as monthly promotions. A popular dish is the tuna sashimi and they also stock local wines. In 2005 Moshi Moshi won the Green Apple Award from The Green Organisation for its campaign to change the way fish are caught and transported. There is a kid's menu and high chairs. Closed on Mondays.

Moshi Moshi © Shaun Oaten

Cabbies' Top Ten Favourite Restaurants

(From The Deckchair poll of 100 local cabbies)

1. China China, 32 Preston Street, Brighton (01273) 328028 **(£)**

...Unpretentious, value for money and tasty Chinese food, served quick. They have high chairs and are very friendly with children too. – Local resident

Anyone for seafood porridge? This vast, efficient restaurant has almost 200 dishes. How to decide? There is every type of Chinese dish you could think of, plus some culinary curiosities. Ever tried deep-fried ice cream? You can here. And if you want something different to swill around your palate, there is chrysanthemum tea and pearl milk tea. Inside, the restaurant is light and airy with wooden furniture and cheerful red décor. Perhaps not the best place for an intimate dinner but great for groups, families, and those in a hurry. (Its takeaway service is very fast – that's probably why it's a favourite with local cabbies). Please note cash-only.

2. Market Diner, 19-21 Circus St, Brighton (01273) 608273 **(£)**
This caff (open through the night) is a local institution, where cabbies sit side by side with wired clubbers and drunken students, and the only sauce that flows is the HP. Open 8.30pm - sunrise.

3. China Garden, 89-91 Preston Street, Brighton (01273) 325124 **(£££)**
The China Garden (established in the city for many years) looks very up market and is immaculate with attentive staff who keep topping up your drinks. It's had a bit of bad press recently – but is still a favourite with the city's cabbies.

4. Aberdeen Steak House, 27-28 Preston Street, Brighton (01273) 326892 **(££)**
Prepare to take a trip back to the 70s with prawn cocktail, steak and chips and crème caramel or sherry trifle on the menu. There's been a change of ownership recently but apparently the old place is still as good as ever (to those in the know). The décor is an arranged marriage of Greek pillars and Scottish tartan....you have been warned!

5. Terre a Terre, (£££)
(see Deckchair Top Ten) **V**

6. Hotel du Vin, 2-6 Ship Street, Brighton (01273) 718588 **(£££)**
With an exceptional wine list, French staff and smart but comfortable bistro style décor you could be forgiven for thinking you were abroad when you dine at the Hotel du Vin. It is part of a chain – but our cabbies voted it in at number six.

7. Browns Bar and Restaurant, 3-4 Duke Street, Brighton (01273) 323501 **(££)**
Another chain, smart but unpretentious, Browns (established 1973) serves up

Donatello's © The Argus

modern British classics like steak, mushroom and Guinness pie with mash and green beans, or grilled whole plaice with lemon butter. It is very popular and has a stylish bar a few doors down.

8. Donatello's, 1-3 Brighton Place, Brighton (01273) 775477 **(£)**
Certainly not the best Italian restaurant in Brighton, but with special offers on two courses for under £8 and smart modern décor, Donatello's has much to recommend itself. Be a bit wary of going for a weekend romantic liaison, as Friday and Saturday nights can get a bit boisterous.

9. One Paston Place, 1 Paston Place, Brighton (01273) 606933 **(£££)**
www.onepastonplace.co.uk
Husband and wife team Francesco Furriello and Rachel Turner – who took over the restaurant in 2004 and achieved great acclaim and a string of awards – have recently decanted to a posh Mayfair eatery. Check the website for latest details.

10. Buffet Island, York Place, Brighton (01273) 698606 **(£)**
From the sublime to the ridiculous; number ten on our cabbies' list is this no-nonsense Chinese restaurant. You can choose from the buffet menu (all you can eat at bargain prices) or select individual dishes from the extensive menu. Although York Parade is not the most salubrious of locations, it's going through a transition at the moment and the restaurant itself has been praised for its cleanliness and bright modern interiors.

Cheaper Restaurants (£)

© Bali Brasserie

Al Rouche, 44 Preston Street, Brighton
(01273) 734810
A Lebanese restaurant par excellence,
according to The Guardian, which
included Al Rouche in its 2006 UK Guide
to World Food. The restaurant is a
welcoming family-run place and mother
is the matriarchal chef! Inside it's
unpretentious-looking, long, narrow and
cosy. A popular dish is the mezze,
consisting of nine (vegetarian or mixed)
starters, for one person or two. The menu
includes delights such as stuffed vine
leaves and baby aubergines stuffed with
walnuts, garlic, chilli, herbs and olive oil.
There are also non-Lebanese dishes, a set
menu and a kid's menu.

Bali Brasserie, First Avenue, Kingsway,
Hove (01273) 323810
www.balibrasserie.com
This odyssey of Malaysian and
Indonesian cuisine at the bottom of a
Hove residential road is way off the
beaten track, but has a loyal following
nonetheless. The décor is 1970s meets
the Far East, with bamboo furniture and
a glitter-tiled bar which has the
distinction of being the longest bar in
the city. The house speciality is the Rice
Table, a four-course extravaganza. There
are also à la carte (including vegetarian
options) and European menus, and a
wide range of desserts. Should you want
a less formal and quicker meal, a
selection of Bali B. fare is available at the
bar. As there is only one sitting,
customers can have the table for as long
as they like. There is live music every
Thursday and Friday. There is also a kid's
menu. Disabled access but no disabled
toilets or baby-changing facilities.

Bankers, 116A Western Road, Brighton
(01273) 328267
This former branch of Lloyds Bank
opened in 1994 and has been popular
ever since, offering both a takeaway
and licensed sit down restaurant.
The extensive menu includes traditional
fish and chip, cooked to order with the
option of fish coated in matzo meal as
opposed to the more traditional batter.
In a 2007 Guardian article, Bankers and
Bardsley's (see below) were voted
amongst the top 30 places to eat in
the UK.

Bardsley's, 22–23a Baker Street,
Brighton (01273) 681256
Passed down through four generations,
Bardsley's opened its doors in 1926 and

Bardsley's © JJ Waller

has always sold some of the best fish and chips in town. With a recently acquired liquor license there's no longer any need to pop down to the nearby pub for a take away pint or bottle of wine to enjoy with your meal. All the fish they serve is line caught and you can enjoy your fish supper fried, poached or grilled. Closed Sundays and Mondays.

Blind Lemon Alley, 41 Middle Street, Brighton (01273) 205151
www.bluescompany.co.uk

It's intimate but very relaxed...
– Local resident

Aptly named, it's rather tucked away and easy to miss, but after visiting you appreciate how Alice in Wonderland must have felt when she grew tall and the rooms appeared to be shrinking around her - you need to bend down to get up the stairs without crunching your head on the beams in this adorable double-fronted cottage. The tables are scrubbed wood and softly lit by candlelight and the place is casual. In other words, the perfect place for a first date and other intimate occasions. The food is good and recalls South America in its range and the Blind Lemon burgers are famously tasty. Here the prices are small and the portions large - a winning combo! There is also live blues entertainment on Sunday nights (book in advance!). NB: at time of going to press the lease is under threat. Check website for details.

BUFFET £4.95
EAT AS MUCH AS YOU LIKE
DAY & NIGHT

OPEN 7 DAYS
BUFFET ONLY
FRI AND SAT
12 NOON TO 12 MIDNIGHT
SUN TO THURS
12 NOON TO ELEVEN

TAKE-AWAY
AVAILABLE

DESSERT FRUIT SALAD | DESSERT INDIAN RICE PUDDING | TARKA DAL | SWEDE & MUSHROOMS | VEGETABLE KORMA | VEGETABLE DHANSAK | CHICK PEAS ALOO | SAAG ALOO | MIXED VEGETABLE CURRY | NAN BREAD | PILAO RICE | SAMOSA | PAKORA

BUFFET £4.95 EAT AS MUCH AS YOU LIKE
OVER 18 ITEMS

Bombay Aloo © David Gray www.imagesbrighton.com

The Blue Man,11 Little East Street, Brighton (01273) 325529
Owner Majid Bensliman first had the idea for his North African restaurant when he was 14 years old (the name comes from a tribe whose indigo robes stain their skin blue). A former professional footballer who represented Algeria, Majid spent much of his youth helping his mother and grandmother in the kitchen, which is where his love of food began. The traditional décor of wall hangings, brass pots and low cushioned seating gives the impression of being inside a Bedouin tent. The menu is not extensive, but typical; meat and vegetarian tagines (cooked slowly in a cone-shaped dish with lots of herbs and spices), sea bass and homemade taguella bread. The desserts are something special too, a mouthwatering sample being baclava honey, almond and rosewater pastries served with dates. The staff are extremely friendly and since moving to their new premises the restaurant now has an alcohol license and even serves North African wines.

Bodega D Tapa, 111 Church Street, Brighton (01273) 674116
www.d-tapa.co.uk
The owner of Bodega D Tapa, Mr Cala, is the man to call if you want good wine. He has only been in Britain two years and both his family and his business partner are wine, liqueur, vinegar and

olive oil producers. He has connections with all the right cellars so the wines change frequently and there's a range of cheeses and meats to complement them. This is one of very few places in Brighton that feels totally like being in another country. It's tiny, bare, rustic and from the outside is an old cottage, yet inside looks nothing like a British eatery.

Bombay Aloo, 39 Ship Street, Brighton (01273) 776038
www.bombay-aloo.co.uk
This is an Indian buffet restaurant with only one price for all you can eat…£4.95 (and even cheaper during Happy Hour Monday-Friday 3.15-5.15pm)! Inside, the décor is fake Tudor. The main buffet is completely vegetarian and includes chickpea aloo, sag aloo, vegetable korma, vegetable curry and the chef's special curry of the day. Desserts are extra and include gulab jamun, spongy milk bon bons marinated in rosewater syrup with cardamom and saffron and kulfi, which is pure frozen milk flavoured with fruits, nuts and herbs.

Buffet Island (see Cabbies' Top Ten)

China China (see Cabbies' Top Ten)

Donatello's (see Cabbies' Top Ten)

E-Kagen, 22-23 Sydney Street, Brighton (01273) 687068
E-Kagen (above Yum Yum) serves no frills, authentic Japanese food. The service is good and there is a friendly, relaxed ambience. However, if you're planning a romantic candle lit dinner, this possibly isn't the place. It is more like a typical cafeteria that you would find in Japan.

Kambi's (see Deckchair Top Ten)

Pablo's, 36 Ship Street, Brighton (01273) 208123
This has to be one of the best-value restaurants in Brighton, with pizza and spaghetti dishes clocking in at £2.50 and Sunday lunch just £5.99. There's also a range of desserts. The place attracts many families so has a stack of high chairs. Popular dishes are the tortelloni funghi and Pablo's salad. This restaurant also specialises in large bookings and can take groups of up to 50.

Planet India (see Deckchair Top Ten)

Red Snapper, 90 Dyke Road, Brighton (01273) 778866
This Thai café and restaurant is warm and relaxed, with a bring-your-own-alcohol policy and no charge for corkage. The interior is wood and in the evening it's low-lit and intimate. Special dishes include gai himmapan, chicken and muh yang pork in a hot, spicy sauce. There is also red snapper, of course, and vegetarian options. At the same time as hitting the mark, nothing about this place says 'Trying too hard'. If it was a person, it would be Kate Moss. Closed for lunch Sundays and Mondays.

Medium Priced Restaurants (££)

Aberdeen Steak House
(see Cabbies' Top Ten)

Al Fresco (see Deckchair Top Ten)

Barry at the Tureen, 31 Upper North Street, Brighton (01273) 328939
A real gem! Forget all the exotic food from desert and jungle that can be found in Brighton, Barry at the Tureen is

Barry at The Tureen © JJ Waller

a truly Brighton establishment that's been around since 1964. The restaurant is welcoming, warm and relaxed. The décor is old-fashioned and technically nothing special, but somehow it all works. Must be something to do with the contrast of the funky-looking Barry (who is the chef and maitre d') and the disarmingly old-fashioned look of the restaurant. His food is predominantly English and well-cooked. Typical dishes include duck legs casseroled with cranberries, onions and red wine and trout fillet sautéed with spring onions, mushrooms, dry vermouth and cream. There's also a range of starters and desserts. Intimate dining rooms on two floors instill the feeling that you are at home rather than out in public. Perhaps this is the secret of its success. Closed Thursdays and Fridays.

Browns Bar and Restaurant
(see Cabbies' Top Ten)

Casa Don Carlos, 5 Union Street, The Lanes (01273) 327177
This is a typical Spanish tapas house with red and white checked tablecloths, candles on the tables and a rustic feel. Small, noisy and welcoming, it would be impossible not to feel cheered by an evening here. This is a place that does what it says on the tin - "the little dishes of Spain" - and doesn't try to be anything else. The chef is Spanish and dishes include the traditional such as gazpacho,

The Dorset © David Gray www.brightonimages.com

tortilla, paella and serrano, and the more adventurous such as rabbit with garlic, wine and chilli. All desserts are home-made. There is no kid's menu or high chairs. Booking in advance is recommended as it gets busy.

The Dorset, 28 North Road, Brighton
(01273) 605423
www.thedorset.co.uk
It's a mish-mash of styles, hard to pin down but strangely appealing. In other words, it's truly Brighton. Too shabby to be upmarket, too nice to be a student hangout. The Dorset is a real fixture with the locals, its mixed crowd including students, office workers, gaggles of girls and people-watchers. In a world of chain restaurants it's good to be somewhere that so obviously hasn't changed in a very long time. You couldn't recreate the uneven floors, the character-laden French café chairs, the old wooden tables or the tortuous layout; the Dorset's lovable raggedness achieves an effortless shabby-chic. And the food? A range of cuisines from across the globe, from breakfast to dinner. On Sundays there is a roast, with a vegetarian nut roast option.

Estia, 3 Hampton Place, Brighton
(01273) 777399
This Greek restaurant is tucked away off Western Road in a former cottage. Inside, the space is light, airy and rather beautiful with its white walls, white floors and fairy lights. There are large mirrors, mahogany chairs and clean, minimalist décor. A major plus point is that all the

Food For Friends © David Gray www.brightonimages.com

meat is organic and locally-produced. A popular dish is kleftiko, slowly-baked lamb shoulder with herbs. On Saturdays there is live music. Estia also does small parties for children and they have high chairs. Closed on Sundays.

Food for Friends, 17-18 Prince Albert Street, Brighton (01273) 202310
www.foodforfriends.com
A Brighton fixture, you can eat healthily here with a clear conscience and still enjoy a touch of luxury in this 19th Century listed building with its calm atmosphere and contemporary yet welcoming decor. The vegetarian menu changes frequently and there are three specials a day. There is also a Sunday lunch with vegetarian and vegan options. Many of the dishes are vegan, gluten-free or low-fat and the restaurant prides itself

on the global influence evident on the menu. All soft drinks are organic and there is a wide range of organic wines. There is a kid's menu with pasta, pizza and veggie burgers, and there are high chairs and changing facilities. On the first Tuesday of every month there is live jazz and on Wednesdays there is relaxing, romantic live music. There's also a takeaway service.

Gars, 19 Prince Albert Street, The Lanes, Brighton (01273) 321321
Gars is a stylish Chinese restaurant in the Lanes with a very loyal following. It serves a mixture of traditional and modern Chinese food (with a few Thai and Japanese dishes too). Gars' special lunch menu for £10 includes a glass of wine and is an ideal opportunity to give it a try without breaking the bank.

Kemp Brasserie, 24-25 St Georges Road, Brighton (01273) 626060
www.kempbrasserie.co.uk

I have taken my trendy son and my 80 year old mother here and both had a lovely time! – Lesley

This unassuming restaurant has a wide range of wines, beers and cocktails and an extensive menu. Located not far from the sea in Kemp Town, like the rest of the district it has an offbeat, funky feel that is very Brighton. The food is good honest British fare with a few nods to places faraway - such as the odd Greek and Cajun dish. Starters include devilled whitebait, sardines and calamari. Mains include caramelised duck breast, and pan-fried monkfish fillet and savoury crepes. As for dessert, chocolate fondue pots, bread and butter pudding, sticky toffee pudding and chocolate fudge cake are on the menu. Brunch is served on Sundays from 11am.

The King and I, 2 Ship Street, Brighton (01273) 773390
www.thekingandi-brighton.co.uk
The unassuming exterior of this restaurant hides a kaleidoscope of colour, texture and sound that makes you forget you are in Brighton. Dark wood, plush red, soft lighting and the gold cutlery and outfits of the staff add up to an unbeatable ambience. The staff are quiet and gracious. Reviews talk about how the chef creates delicate, aromatic flavours without burning the mouths of his customers, and we're not

about to disagree. Starters include thao hoo tod, fried bean curd with chilli sauce and peanut, and meek rod (crispy noodles flavoured with tamarind sauce). For mains, try the jungle curry, or gang pha.

La Capannina, 15 Madeira Place, Brighton (01273) 680839
It doesn't look much from the outside, but inside there is a soaring vaulted ceiling, an open fire and lots of creamy old oak wood. This place is reminiscent of an upmarket ski lodge and Kemp Town recedes far into the background once you step inside. The menu serves up simple pizzas and Italian grub, nothing too wild or fanciful. Word of mouth recommendation is consistently good. Think about booking because it's quite small and gets busy.

Lee Cottage, 6b Queens Road, Brighton (01273) 327643
www.leecottage.co.uk
This family run restaurant serves tasty Cantonese, Szechuan and Peking cuisine in an unpretentious upstairs dining area. Visit their website for Sunday specials and set menu offers.

Mai Ped Ped Ped, 11 Market Street, Brighton (01273) 737373
Set in a beautifully cosy old house in one of Brighton's nicest squares, the food and service at this restaurant is variable although, if you pick the right night, both can be excellent! The menu includes tapas, featuring stuffed squid in basil and chilli sauce and hiccup duck (yep, typed it

right) - a spasm in your diaphragm. Mains include gra tiam, chicken and prawns sautéed with garlic and covered in golden crisp garlic flake, and red duck curry. There is also an excellent and cheap lunch menu in the winter. The attractive interior is all pale wood with crisp white tablecloths and candles. It's up to you if you choose to play the restaurant lottery and see if your night is a good one!

Mint, 42 Meeting House Lane, Brighton (01273) 323824

On Fridays they have a resident astrologer who is spookily good....and the food is pretty scrumptious too. – Local resident

Tucked away in the Lanes in an old bow-fronted cottage - you can easily miss it, which would be a shame - Mint can be a lively place on Thursday and Saturday evenings, when there is live music. Boasting rustic tables in a chocolate-box setting, it's open for breakfast, lunch and dinner so there's sure to be something on the menu for everyone. The café menu has nods to Greece, Spain and the Far East; quite a good selection for a

small place, but the main draw here is the great atmosphere.

Momma Cherri's Big House,
2-3 Little East Street, Brighton
(01273) 325305
www.mommacherri.co.uk
Gordon Ramsay helped put Momma and her soul food on the map. So whether it's Southern-style okra gumbo you're after or a glimpse of Momma herself, head on down to the big house and let her team put a smile on your face!

Moshi Moshi (see Deckchair Top Ten)

Muang Thai, 77 St James's Street, Brighton (01273) 605223
The oldest Thai restaurant in Brighton, Muang Thai has been open for 20 years. Authentic seating - raised platform with low tables and padded cushions – is a nice touch. All the wood is mahogany, lending the place a dark, mysterious feel and the tables are Thai spice tables. The herbs used in cooking are ordered in several times a week so they are fresh and not hanging around in a hot kitchen. Popular dishes are the satay and the 'special mixed hoard of muang thai'. Where else in Brighton can you order a hoard? Like it, like it!

Murasaki, 115 Dyke Road, Brighton
(01273) 326231
A very friendly intimate Japanese café/restaurant just off Seven Dials, serving small tapas-type dishes and different sorts of sushi. Well-regarded and reasonably-priced.

Muang Thai publicity shot © The Argus

Prompt Corner © JJ Waller

Nou Nou, 120 St. George's Road, Brighton (01273) 682200
A slice of North Africa with an expensive-looking interior, and downstairs there is an intimate bar with low seating and lots of cushions; it's certainly a place to go for something different. If a flavour of the desert is what you want, this is a good place to impress as it's probably the most luxurious restaurant devoted to this region of the world in Brighton. Good service too. The menu includes rabbit, monkfish and sea bass tagines, lots of lamb and Moroccan rice.

Brighton Pagoda, Brighton Marina (01273) 819053
www.brightonpagoda.co.uk
Pagoda is an old mahogany Chinese boat, like a wide barge with a roof. It's Brighton's only floating restaurant and is moored in the Marina. Inside, the wood is very old and the atmosphere romantic. The gradient of the gangway up to the restaurant varies depending on how high the tide is. The menu is standard Chinese fare with a few surprises thrown in for good measure. This is a perfect place for a romantic date, Sunday lunch, or a bring-the-parents outing. Possibly not your first choice for a raucous night out.

Pintxo People (see Deckchair Top Ten)

Prompt Corner, 36 Montpelier Road, Brighton (01273) 737624
www.promptcorner.com
This is a theatrical restaurant complete with obligatory ghost. Small and cosy, its

The Regency © JJ Waller

walls are filled with images of Hollywood and the restaurant is named after the part of the theatre where the prompter sits. Prompt Corner is a real Brighton fixture. The menu (which has been criticised in some reviews for being a bit Seventies) is laid out in acts, Act I for starters and so on. The beef wellington and the stroganoff are widely eulogised. Desserts are a simple selection of homemade sweets, sorbets and ice creams. In a world where chefs compete to produce ever more exotic and outlandish menus, Prompt Corner stays resolutely proud of its culinary base.

(although it does help, being a seafood restaurant) as there are alternative options. Locally-caught fish is the Regency's speciality and it's the best place in town to try simple, grilled fish of all types. There is a children's menu too. Fish-mad or a fish-dodger, this place is a Brighton institution and you have no right to call yourself a Brightonian until you've set foot in here.

Riddle and Finns, 12b Meeting House Lane, Brighton and 129 Church Road, Hove (01273) 323008/721667 www.riddleandfinns.co.uk
From the simplicity of pan fried scallops to the decadence of champagne caviar and oysters, this luxurious eatery serves up some of the freshest seafood in the city. The a la carte isn't cheap, but they have a special lunch deal which is quite reasonable. You can even take home the catch of the day from their wet fish counter!

Maybe they have an inkling that not everyone wants to pay high prices to eat spangled sharkfish with stuffed gills served on a bed of glazed hay. Excellent! Closed on Mondays.

The Regency, 131 King's Road, Brighton (01273) 325014
www.theregencyrestaurant.co.uk
One of Brighton's grand old eateries! Everyone knows about it, but we had to put it in out of respect. It has been open since the Thirties so they must be doing something right. You don't have to be fish-mad to dine at the Regency

Expensive Restaurants (£££)

The China Garden
(see Deckchair Top Ten)

Due South (see Deckchair Top Ten)

The Gingerman (see Deckchair Top Ten)

Havana, 33 Duke Street, Brighton
(01273) 773388
If you feel like spoiling yourself (money no object) you should book a table at Havana. The beautiful cream and mahogany interior, attentive staff and tantalizing menu afford this restaurant a plush, colonial air. The emphasis here is on fine dining and impeccable service and this is also reflected in the stylish, well stocked bar…perfect for that special occasion.

Hotel du Vin (see Cabbie's Top Ten)

Indian Summer, 69 East Street, Brighton and 5 Victoria Terrace, Kingsway, Hove
(01273) 711001/773090
www.indian-summer.org.uk
This fragrant Indian restaurant is rather beautiful in a minimalist, rustic-wood kind of way. I was informed they don't do curry because curries are from Bangladesh, not India, and this is real Indian cuisine. The menu changes every three months, and much of their menu is suitable for vegans and is gluten-free. The menu includes a very good value lunch deal: £10 for two courses. The dinner menu includes dishes such as malai murgh, tender chicken breast marinated in cheese and hung yoghurt

© Sevendials Restaurant

served with a creamy malai sauce. There's no kid's menu but the chef will make dishes smaller and milder. There are high chairs but no baby-changing facilities. The restaurant takes part in the Streetsmart campaign to donate money to the homeless.

The Real Eating Company, 86-87 Western Road, Hove (01273) 221444 www.real-eating.co.uk
With the emphasis on real food the café's ethos is to source the best local products available. They call themselves a deli/café and have a loyal clientele, serving breakfast lunch and dinner with a specials board that changes daily. The upstairs deli serves excellent British cheeses and it

is reassuring to see the kitchen also on the first floor cooking everything to order. The only downside is that the service could be a bit sharper. (They also have branches at Lewes and Horsham).

Sevendials Restaurant, 1 Buckingham Place, Seven Dials, Brighton (01273) 885555
Previously a Lloyds Bank and then a Burger King, Sevendials has had its share of good national reviews for its modern European cuisine, and often has summer eating, drinking and music on its terrace - which suffers slightly from its situation right on the roundabout.

Terre a Terre (see Deckchair Top Ten)

Cafés and Tea Rooms

My favourite was Ma Egan's, … situated in Stone Street off Preston Street. It was little more than a long hut with tables each side and a kitchen at one end….. On entering, you would call out, "Mug (or cup) of tea and one and one," followed by the number of your party and then the table number. Tea was two old pence for a mug or one and a half pence for a cup. 'One and one' was a slice of bread and butter and a slice of bread and dripping with thick brown gravy on top.
Tim Wren – Flying Sparks (QueenSpark Books, 1998)

The Top Ten Cafés
(As voted in The Deckchair Poll)

1. Red Roaster, 1d St James's Street, Brighton (01273) 686668

Couches, newspapers, friendly staff, loyalty cards and lovely coffee.
– Local resident

As its name suggests this café at the bottom of St James's Street roasts its own coffee beans for use in the café and to take away. Excellent coffee and a lively caffeinated atmosphere.

2. The Sanctuary, 51-55 Brunswick Street, Hove (01273) 770002

The Sanctuary Café is a chilled out funky place to sit and drink a glass of wine, eat some healthy food and read a paper. It is open late too, which is always a bonus!
– Local resident

Having recently changed hands the new owners seem to be maintaining the high standard of food and drink that people have come to expect from this Hove café. The décor is less eccentric than once it was, but the beautiful airy building is still a lovely place to relax.

3. Bill's, The Depot, 11 North Road, Brighton (01273) 692894
www.billsproducestore.co.uk
Quite forbidding from the outside (it used to be a bus depot) you'd never guess that Bill's is one of Brighton's most original and delicious eating spaces. Each morning the doors swing open to reveal a double-decker high space that's part eatery part food market and packed to bursting with organic produce. Undeniably rustic, you half-expect to come out and find the streets of Brighton grassed over and roaming with farm animals. The menu is simple and

The Pavilion Gardens Café © David Gray

Bill's © JJ Waller

delicious, with uncomplicated dishes such as grilled vine tomatoes on toast, crumpets, buttermilk pancakes and the best bacon sandwich I've ever eaten! There is also a selection of organic wines and cocktails. One word of caution though, wrap up in winter as those stable-like doors do let in the cold. There are baby-changing facilities and toilets for disabled customers.

4. Pavilion Gardens Café, Royal Pavilion Grounds, New Road, Brighton
Fantastic cake, friendly staff, perfect location. – Sonja

At first glance this looks simply like a nice café in the gardens of the Pavilion, but its heritage stretches back to a 1920s stall selling cockles, mussels and whelks by the sea. This stall and a nearby pub was owned by the current Café owner's great-grandparents. His grandfather,

Mr T, then owned two stalls under the Arches selling ice cream, cakes etc. He would bring his pies, breads and cakes down to the sea in a wheelbarrow from Elm Grove. If the weather was bad, much of it was thrown to the fish on the Sunday night. And so it was that Mr T. began baking his own cakes. If it wasn't for the war, perhaps the operation would still be down by the beach. However, the stall had to close in order to make way for beach reinforcements in case of invaders, the result being that the Pavilion Gardens Café was born. Today, it is run by Mr T's descendants, and the family has now held the lease for approaching 70 years. A Brighton fixture, the café was almost closed down in 1989 by the Brighton Tourism Council Committee demanding the site owners give up their lease after almost 50 years. But there was a public outcry. A good thing too: in the summer you can hardly

Red Roaster © Henry Law

The Pavilion Gardens Café © David Gray

The Meeting Place © David Gray

get near the place it's so popular, and it's almost as full on cold days when the sun's out, or indeed on any day that's not bitterly cold or rainy. Today the café has given up its whelks, mussels and cockles, and now sells salads, sandwiches, baguettes, cakes, baked potatoes, teas, coffees etc. There is a space for artists to show or perform their work, and the Gardens are never dull in the summer.

5. The Mock Turtle, 4 Pool Valley, Brighton (01273) 327380.
This tea room is a wonderful place to bring foreign visitors to Brighton as it has a very traditional English atmosphere. Lots of different teas, fabulous home-made cakes and snacks served on a variety of pretty china.

6. Mad Hatter, 35 Montpelier Road, Brighton (01273) 722279
People who love this café always seem to comment on the lovely staff and the big windows (a legacy of the building's former incarnation as Timothy Whites many years ago). The coffee and cake seem pretty popular too.

7. The Meeting Place, Kingsway, Hove (01273) 738391
The serving hatch is in Brighton, the seating area is in Hove! It's worthwhile stopping for a home made cake and a Rombouts coffee, but don't miss your order number being called, as the server gets increasingly irate…

8. The Cowley Club, 12 London Road Brighton (01273) 696104

A co-operatively run social centre offering affordable vegan meals as an alternative to fast food outlets. It also houses a radical bookshop with titles on everything from Allotment Gardening to the Zapatistas…and has live music from local bands. – Andrew

Holding its own near the newly opened Costa on London Road, the Cowley Club café offers simple food and drink at far cheaper prices.

9. Wai Kika Moo Kau, 11a Kensington Gardens, Brighton (01273) 671117
A popular vegetarian haunt in the North Laine. Big portions and friendly staff, though vegans felt they weren't catered for as well as their veggie counterparts.

10. Toast, 38 Trafalgar Street Brighton (01273) 626888
A great place to stop for tea, toast and a read of the papers on the way to the station. Good value and popular with the Trafalgar Street workers for made-to-order takeaway sandwiches too.

The Deckchair pick of the rest...

The Dumb Waiter, 28 Sydney St, Brighton (01273) 602526
Don't be fooled by the brightly coloured, quirky décor - the Dumb Waiter is an old style caff. It serves good value veggie and non-veggie food in portions hearty enough to satisfy the hungriest student.

The Gallery Café, Brighton Museum, Royal Pavilion Gardens (01273) 290900
The café is located on the balcony overlooking the furniture exhibits in the main hall. You can drink tea served from art deco style pots and enjoy cakes and light lunches in the calm atmosphere and subdued lighting of the gallery. Closed on Mondays.

Infinity Café, 50 Gardner Street, Brighton (01273) 670743
A haven for serious veggies, The Infinity Café serves up delicious organic food in a light and contemporary atmosphere. Great people watching from the upstairs window too!

I have so many dietary requirements and Infinity Foods Café cater for them all!
– Local resident

Inside Out, 95 Gloucester Road, Brighton (01273) 692912
A popular café for a Saturday breakfast in the North Laine. Sit outside amongst the Gaudi-esque mosaics and watch the people go by.

La Gigo Gi, 24 New Road, Brighton (01273) 687753
Owner Giovanni used to own and run the wonderful Italian Deli at Seven Dials, so it's a promising start for this snappy little Italian Sandwich Bar which has recently opened in New Road, directly opposite Carluccio's.

Louis' Beach Café, Kings Road Arches, Brighton (01273) 771555
With a prime location on the seafront, Louis' also has a charming interior (a refurbished fisherman's arch) and always plays good tunes. However the service really lets it down, which is a great shame because it used to be *the* place for coffee on Brighton prom.

Marrocco's, King's Esplanade, Hove (01273) 203764

…a fantastic mix of old school American diner and Italian bistro. You can have an authentic Italian feast or pop in for an ice cream float. You can buy one cup of tea and stay all day if you like! – Lucy

Not an upmarket North African restaurant, but a shabby beach café. The location is fantastic, right by the water on a sweep of wide prom, and late on a wintry, sunny afternoon in early March it still teems with business; this is probably the dingiest caff around, but it pretty much has a monopoly on passing trade. It serves the usual beach-type fare: burgers, pizzas, crisps and salads, and a really great range of ice creams. Kids get a free pizza when a large one is ordered.

Nia, 87–88 Trafalgar Street, Brighton (01273) 462777
You can now eat breakfast lunch and dinner at this serene and stylish café. The food is good but some people commented that the service can be slow and a little eccentric.

Off Beat, 37-38 Sydney St, Brighton (01273) 604206
Walk into the Offbeat café and you might start wondering where Cliff and his mates are. Designed to look like a Fifties coffee bar this retro café is the perfect place to perch on a high stool and drink a cappuccino Daddy–o!

Rock-Ola, 29 Tidy Street (01273) 673744 (see page 125)

Steamers, 35 Ship Street, Brighton (01273) 227705 (upstairs at Steamer Trading Cookshop)
A hidden gem in the heart of the city. Located on the first floor of this wonderfully chic cookshop, you'll always find a seat in this café. If it's lunch you're after, there isn't a big selection, but they serve an excellent cup of tea or coffee and have a decent range of cakes and biscuits.

Tallula's Tea Rooms, 9 Hampton Place, Brighton (01273) 710529

A fantastic choice of teas and coffees that are served in teapots and cafetieres, great cakes and cream teas and they have starched white table cloths and jazz on in the background. – Local resident

Delightful cottagey tea rooms tucked away in a side street off the busy Western Road, you wouldn't know Tallula's was there unless someone had bothered to let you in on the secret. They serve full meals as well as English tearoom fare, and there is a really impressive range of teas and coffees. A nice environment and a bit of peace and quiet off a busy road.

Marrocco's © David Gray www.brightonimages.com

03

Drinking in Brighton & Hove

In a city that's awash with bars and pubs here's a selection of watering holes that encapsulate Brighton & Hove's colourful past and unique character. Whether you're visiting for the first time or you've lived here for fifty years, your next great drink in this town could be just around the corner.....

The City's Top Ten Pubs

(as voted in The Deckchair Poll)

Dark Star ales on tap at the Evening Star © JJ Waller

1. The George
(see Best For Food)

2. The Great Eastern
(see Best Seasonal Pubs)

3. The Basket Makers
(see Best For Food)

4. Preston Park Tavern
(see Best For Food)

5. The Regency
(see Best Sunday Roasts)

6. The Evening Star
(see Three Pubs With A Story)

7. The Battle of Trafalgar
(see Best Seasonal Pubs)

8. The Colonnade
(see Best Seasonal Pubs)

9· The Crescent
(see Best Pub Quizzes)

10. The Eagle
(see Best Seasonal Pubs)

Historical Pubs

Brighton has a reputation for knowing how to have a good time. Ever since Richard Russell 'Dr Brighton' (a resident of nearby Lewes) published his paper in 1750 claiming bathing in seawater was good for your health, people began flocking here. At least two pubs claim the title of Brighton's oldest pub, with both buildings dating back to the 1500s.

The Druids Head at 9, Brighton Place, is named after the discovery, a couple of centuries ago, of a stone circle nearby which was believed to be of Druid origin. It is thought the pub came into existence in the 17th Century, when the smuggling of liquor and other hard to come by commodities was at its height.

Allegedly, secret tunnels were built from there down to the beach. Today the pub still stands in the heart of the lanes, newly refurbished but keeping its historic charm with dark wood panelling, real ales and a refreshing lack of all things fruit machine like.

The Cricketers, on Black Lion Street, not far from the Druids, is more widely recognised as Brighton's oldest tavern. A haven for fishermen in the 17th Century, the pub was originally known as the *Last and Fishcart* and renamed in the 18th Century when a local cricket legend became landlord. Upstairs the Greene Room pays tribute to its namesake Graham Greene. With its

The Druids Head dates from the 17th Century © David Gray

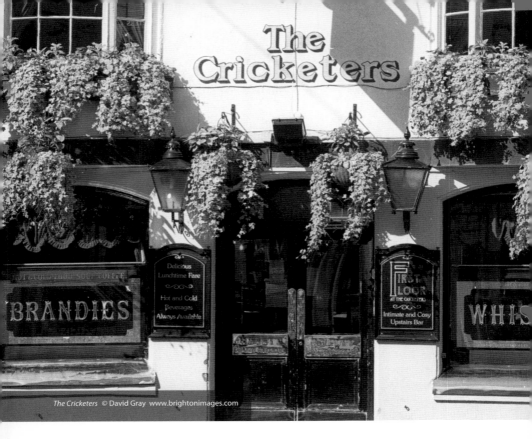

The Cricketers © David Gray www.brightonimages.com

lush red carpets and excess of brass and mirrors, stepping through the doors is like entering a true Victorian establishment. The pub serves real ales and whiskies and reasonably priced lunchtime food. Although owned by the Golden Lion Group it doesn't feel as though it's part of a chain.

Another pub of historical interest is the **Queensbury Arms**, situated the sea end of Queensbury Mews. It has a plaque outside stating that it's the smallest pub in Brighton. Known affectionately as 'the Hole in the Wall', this nickname comes from when the

Royal Fusiliers were stationed nearby during the early days of the First World War and reputedly served drinks through a gap in the pub's wall. Now serving real ales and the usual spirits, wines and lagers through two small rooms either side of the bar, the pub showcases signed photographs of theatre performers and artists who have drunk there. Laurence Olivier is rumoured to have drunk half a bottle of champagne in the tiny pub, dressed scruffily and wearing sunglasses to avoid recognition!

Nurses & NHS Workers Favourite Pubs

We polled 50 nurses and NHS workers asking them to tell us their favourite local pubs. It seems the St George's Inn in Sudeley Street is their favourite haunt and the place they go after work, although some preferred the Barley Mow down the road. Several complained that on NHS wages they couldn't afford to go to pubs. Also in the running were some of the big beasts of West Street like Yates's Wine Lodge and Wetherspoons (rather them than us!). Here are their top five:

1. St George's Inn
(formerly the Sudeley Arms) Sudeley Street, Brighton (01273) 694265
1,386 different sausage, mash and gravy combinations (just like its sister pub, the Shakespeare's Head) barbeques in the summer and a constant Happy Hour for NHS staff are probably the reasons that make this number one on our nurses' list.

2. The Barley Mow
92 St George Street, Brighton (01273) 682259
Nothing beats a cold night outside whilst being inside with a roaring open fire. Add a fine selection of drinks and a cracking Sunday roast and it makes the trek up to Kemptown so worth it. It's like a night out in your living room. Grab a paper and do the crossword, grab some friends and do the quiz or one of the many board games on offer. Just make sure you get a seat next to the fire and all will be right with the world.

3. King and Queen
13 Marlborough Place, Brighton (01273) 607207
A huge mock Tudor pub featuring two big TV screens. If it were a person you might describe it as loud, lewd and lairy…..whatever floats your boat.

4. Sidewinder
65 Upper St James's Street, Brighton (01273) 679927
A very popular bar with a friendly, laid-back atmosphere. They also serve scrumpy cider on tap; could that be why the nurses liked it?

5. Royal Pavilion Tavern
7 Castle Square, Brighton (01273) 827641
Known locally as The Pav Tav, it looks like a refurbished Berni Inn but does have a good indie club upstairs.

© David Gray www.brightonimages.com

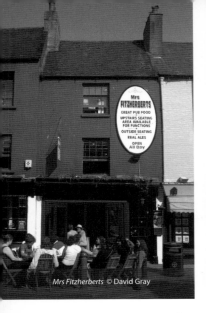

Mrs Fitzherberts © David Gray

The Fortune of War © Richard Rutter

Best Seasonal Pubs

Let's be honest, unless you have the best local in the world (or are *very* lazy) the weather usually dictates the kind of pub you're in the mood for. Whether it's a sundeck to drink very cold beer on or a sofa next to a roaring fire with real ale served in jugs, Brighton & Hove has it all and more. Here are The Deckchair's recommendations for the best drinking establishments in town to embrace (or determinedly deny) our diverse weather system.

Summer Breeziness

What better way is there to enjoy summer in Brighton & Hove than people-watching with a cold beer in your hand? Or relaxing in a secluded pub garden with a cold beer in your hand? Or alternatively, reading the paper al fresco with a cold beer in your hand…you get the picture.

Mrs Fitzherberts
New Road, Brighton (01273) 682401
Known to the locals as Fitz's, this humble pub doubles in size in the summer when its tables and chairs spill out onto the recently pedestrianised New Road. Perfect for meeting your friends, eyeing the customers of the nearby Mash Tun and Waggon and Horses, enjoying the harassment of passing shoppers and generally lazing in the sun. They even open up the front sliding doors to give you maximum access to the bar from all directions. How thoughtful.

The Fortune of War
157 Kings Road Arches, Brighton Seafront (01273) 205065
A pub rather than a bar, this is one of the busiest seafront summer watering holes. Serving drinks in plastic cups if you choose to sit on the beach instead of the

© David Gray www.brightonimages.com

benches provided, the Fortune's nautical theme and proximity to the sea make you feel like you're on holiday even if you only live down the road. Excellent for the first Pimms of the summer.

The Battle of Trafalgar
34 Guildford Road, Brighton
(01273) 327997
This pub's trump card is that its beer garden remains a sun trap long after others have been put in the shade. With so many tables crammed in the garden it can get a little friendly. Get here early, nab a table, spread out a newspaper and enjoy those all-too-brief Brighton & Hove summers.

The Office
8 Sydney Street, Brighton
(01273) 609134
With the doors propped open in the summer it's always tempting to wander off the street and into this little pub offering very cold beers and big tables in the windows. Outside is a two-tiered garden offering a great suntrap and, for when that gets too much, a slightly bigger area covered with creeping vines which give you a cool sun-dappled shade. There always seems to be packs of cards lying around on the tables inviting you to spend a couple of lazy hours challenging your friends to a not-too-strenuous game. Or maybe they're a clever marketing ploy to encourage drinking games?

Winter Coziness

If you must venture outside in the winter months make it somewhere warm and cosy where you can forget about the world outside…

The Ancient Mariner
59 Rutland Road, Hove (01273) 748595
A whole room of sofas to be fought over, and, when it gets slightly warmer (or now the smoking ban's in force), huge

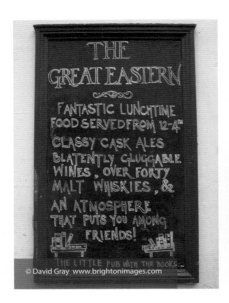

© David Gray www.brightonimages.com

© David Gray www.brightonimages.com

outdoor heaters in the garden make The Mariner a haven in any kind of weather. The recent take-over by Bob the Sausage has brought with it a menu of sausage and mash to die for. Not just any sausage and mash mind, but any possible imagining of sausage (veggie included), mash (who knew how many vegetables could be mashed?) and gravy to warm the very cockles of your sea-breeze frozen heart.

The Colonnade

10 New Road, Brighton (01273) 328728
Overflowing with theatrical memorabilia, the Colonnade is a wonderfully evocative old style pub. It gets quite crowded at interval time (as it's next door to the Theatre Royal) but that just adds to the character.

The Eagle

125 Gloucester Road, Brighton
(01273) 607765
This pub could easily make it onto both summer and winter lists. Its warm tones, pine furniture and fresh flowers create an airy but homely atmosphere with great food.

I like The Eagle so much because it is one of the few bars in Brighton that plays indie rock most of the time – Spiro

minimalist décor in this old style boozer. The old wooden panelling and shelves are filled with books and it serves a wide selection of beers (including guest ales that change weekly) and whiskeys (scotch, bourbon, you name it…) help you keep warm as you settle in for the night.

The Bristol Bar
Paston Place, Brighton (01273) 605687
Although situated in deepest darkest Kemptown, your trip will be rewarded by one of the best pub views of the sea in town, and the guarantee of a seat. A pub – and clientele – of character.

Three Pubs With A Story

The Evening Star/Dark Star Brewery
56 Surrey Street, Brighton
(01273) 328931
This tiny pub with its scrubbed wooden floor and heavy wooden furniture gives a rustic welcome to all who visit. Overflowing with steam engine paraphernalia, it is alleged (falsely apparently) that the pub was named after the last steam locomotive to be built in England. This is where you go for the best beer in Sussex. The Evening Star is famous for spawning the Dark Star brewery from its very own cellars. The pub was awarded the CAMRA (Campaign for Real Ale) Sussex and Surrey Regional pub of the Year award in

The Farm
13 Farm Road, Hove (01273) 325902
The fairy light strewn front windows and real log fire make this pub perfect for a cosy night out. Spend the evening snuggled by the fire on one of the comfy sofas sampling a whiskey or three…perfect.

The Great Eastern
103 Trafalgar Street, Brighton
(01273) 685681
You won't find trendy artwork or

The Evening Star © JJ Waller

2005 and it's easy to see why. It offers a large rotating selection of house beers as well as a constantly changing selection of Dark Star beers and guest ales and at least one organic lager always on tap.

In 1994, with half the cellar occupied by a 'micro-brewery', The Evening Star started brewing its own beer. It soon became apparent they couldn't keep up with the growing demands, not just from their ever-thirsty and curious customers but from other pubs requesting their unique talents as guest ales. In 2001 the brewery relocated to Ansty near Haywards Heath, from where it still supplies a selection of beers to the Evening Star as well as selling direct to other pubs. Dark Star has gone on to be named Best Brewery in England and 84th

in the world by American website ratebeer.com.

For updates on the latest guest ales and Dark Star offerings as well as live music performed at the Evening Star check their website: www.eveningstarbrighton.co.uk

For information on the Dark Star Brewery and where you can buy their ales visit www.darkstarbrewing.co.uk

The Earth and Stars

26 Windsor Street, Brighton
(01273) 722879
The Earth and Stars opened in 2001 as Brighton's first all singing, all dancing eco-friendly pub. Owned by Brighton company Zelgrain, it boasts solar powered panelling for all the pub's hot water, recycled waste and fair trade

The Earth and Stars © JJ Waller

renewable energy sources for their electricity. It also offers a wide range of organic and locally sourced drinks, including lager, wine, spirits and cider (try the pear!), although has a disappointingly small range of real ales. Still, it's not every day you get to feel like you're doing your bit for environmental awareness when you buy a round. Before you start to feel a little sickened by all this well-being they do sell cigarettes behind the bar; organic ones, naturally. The food menu, though small, offers typical pub food, as organic and locally sourced as possible, including excellent vegetarian and vegan options. The Sunday roasts are recommended.

The atmosphere, usually fairly mellow during the week, livens up with the resident DJs at the weekend, entertaining a mixed crowd that are quite hard to pigeonhole. It's a genuinely delightful pub, small with friendly staff, attractively decked out with mis-matched wooden furniture and situated in the heart of town. A true Brighton experience not to be missed. *Food served Monday to Thursday, 12-3pm and 5-8pm. Friday – Sunday 12-5pm.*

The Robin Hood
3 Norfolk Place, Brighton (01273) 325645
The Robin Hood has the honour and notoriety of being Britain's first 'Peoples Pub', a concept thought up by Brighton entrepreneurs Martin Webb and Neil Hayward. The idea is to create pubs that are commercially viable with the profit given back to the community. Recognising that pubs are often the

Fun and games at The Robin Hood © JJ Waller

heart of British social life they believe this to be a unique venture in charity fundraising for specific areas (the more successful the pub, the more money there is to award to local groups) whilst also offering a traditional but contemporary and quality venue.

The Robin Hood is the blueprint for People's Pubs but stands its ground as one of Brighton's busiest and most popular establishments. Half of the inside looks like a normal pub, rough wooden tables and interesting art on the walls. The other half looks like you've stumbled into somebody's front room. There's carpet and stripy wallpaper, and armchairs and sofas are arranged with convenient old style reading lamps. With a selection of beers on offer and a pizza oven, the pub caters for most tastes. It also offers free internet access and wireless for those with laptops. The aim is to have a chain of these pubs across the land, not quite stealing from the rich and giving to the poor but enabling people to give back to their community in a way far more enjoyable than most people could imagine.

Best For Food

Tobacco tins at the Basketmakers © JJ Waller

The Basketmakers
12 Gloucester Road, Brighton
(01273) 689006
This pub wears its history proudly, from the days when the mods and rockers hung out here. It doesn't have a jukebox, only low-key eclectic music and the buzz of happy drinkers. The two things this pub is famous for (three if you count the fact that most locals would rather not tell you where it is) are its whiskeys and its tobacco tins - hundreds of the latter adorn the walls. Who knows how long they've been there or how the tradition started but leaving a message is a must. The bar is piled high with an assortment of bottles, optics, tankards, beer mats and other drink-related paraphernalia. A good selection of real ales, huge selection of spirits as well as award winning home-cooked pub food served by friendly staff keep the punters coming back for more.

The Chimney House
28 Upper Hamilton Road (01273) 556708
Tucked away off the Old Shoreham Road beyond Seven Dials, The Chimney House was the city's first real gastro pub. The light spacious interior features an open-plan kitchen where you can watch the chefs at work. If you fancy the sound of venison pie and chips with homemade ketchup or hill-reared Highland Blackface lamb loin chops with potato rosti and savoy cabbage you're in for a treat. They also serve good fish dishes and cater for veggies. Incidentally, this was the first pub in the city to be totally non-smoking (well before the ban was in place). Open seven days a week for lunch and dinner, tables are allocated on a first come first served basis.

The George
5 Trafalgar Street, Brighton
(01273) 681055
A studenty atmosphere, large portions and friendly service, sums up the George - and it's the only totally veggie pub in the city. Four reasons that make The George a worthy member of the Deckchair good food list.

The Greys in Hanover © David Gray www.brightonimages.com

Ginger Pig

3 Hove Street, Hove (01273) 736123
This gastro pub is owned by Ben and
Pamela McKellar who also own The
Ginger Man and Drakes. Locals have
raved about the food and, whilst it isn't
cheap, it is slightly more affordable than
their other two restaurants. Due to its
popularity and the fact that you can't
book – get there early or you might not
get a table. Open: Monday to Saturday
for lunch and dinner and 12.30pm to
4:00pm on Sundays.

The Greys

(see Best Sunday Roasts)

The Hop Poles, 13 Middle Street,
Brighton (01273) 710444
This pub (sister pub to the Eagle) is
popular with students and gets very
busy. The food is hearty pub fare and
veggies are well catered for.

Preston Park Tavern

88 Havelock Road, Brighton
(01273) 542271
In the heart of Fiveways this is yet
another gastro pub that makes the
Deckchair good food list. The menu is
concise and seasonal and their wine list
is similarly thoughtful. There is also a
spacious garden for more relaxed
dining. Open: Monday to Saturday for
lunch and dinner and food is served
from 12.30pm to 6:00pm on Sundays.

The best hangover cure in town at the The Greys © David Gray

Best Sunday Roasts

Brighton in particular has developed a Sunday Roast culture all of its own, and most pubs offer nutritional respite from the post-Saturday hangover until late in the afternoon. Good Sunday chefs often move from pub to pub when a better offer comes along, but the following can be relied upon to satisfy your meat and veggie needs, serving up consistently good Sunday lunches.

The Regency Tavern
32-34 Russell Square (01273) 325652
Refined and genteel, and worth visiting for the kitsch décor alone.

The Greys
105 Southover Street (01273) 680734
Great atmosphere and Egon Ronay-listed; serving only from12 - 3pm and very popular, so get there early. Spats has gone but the owner's insistence for quality should ensure they find a worthy replacement. *The Greys is a friendly local with great beer and interesting music.* – Jamie

The Yeoman
7 Guildford Road (01273) 327985
Always packed, so get in early for a slightly posher take on the traditional trimmings.

The Open House
146 Springfield Road (01273) 880102
Large and airy, with a lovely garden area for those sunny days.

Brighton Rocks
6 Rock Place (01273) 601139
Tucked away in a small mews off the seafront, this New England inspired bar serves award winning cocktails and a famous Sunday lunch.

Favourite Gay Pubs

'The 42 Club did gay shows at the Co-op hall in London Road. They did it for charity, for St John's Ambulance or something like that. A drag show and a gay show…. They had 'Brighton Gay', 'Brighton Gayer', 'Brighton Gayest'. There was a wonderful opening number, with everyone dressed as the Roman Legion, 'Tramp, tramp, tramp, the boys are out to camp,' and wonderfully witty numbers.' (Daring Hearts: Lesbian and Gay Lives of 50's and 60's Brighton–QueenSpark Books,1992)

Although all the pubs listed in this section should be gay friendly, here are a few that most definitely are!

The Bedford Tavern

30 Western Street, Hove
(01273) 739465
A quiet gay-friendly mixed pub in Hove.

Brighton Rocks

(see Best Sunday Roasts)

The Brighton Tavern

100 Gloucester Road, Brighton
(01273) 680365
A convivial mixed pub situated just two minutes walk from the station in the North Laine area. Quite lively with regular parties and cabaret.

Charles Street

Marine Parade, Brighton (01273 624091)
This trendy pub/bar is within easy reach of all the nearby gay clubs. It has a pretty outside terrace and great food.

Marine Tavern

13 Broad Street, Brighton
(01273) 681284
A proper local, this jolly little pub offers fun every night of the week with regular quiz nights on Tuesdays.

Queens Arms

7 George Street, Brighton
(01273) 696873
Live entertainment every night of the week ensures this stalwart of the gay scene keeps its popularity crown.

Queensbury Arms

Queensbury Mews, Brighton
(01273) 328159
With an older crowd, this tiny, very friendly pub is just off the seafront and perfect for a quiet drink.

The Marlborough

4 Princes Street, Brighton
(01273) 570028
This intimate two-bar pub with a small theatre upstairs is frequented mostly by women. It has a pool table and a friendly relaxed atmosphere.

Legends

31-32 Marine Parade, Brighton
(01273) 624462
Attached to Legends Hotel, the refurbished bar, weekly cabaret, a fantastic terrace and great views attracts a mixed crowd.

The Regency (see Best Sunday Roasts)

Best Pub Quizzes

All in Brighton, and in no particular order…

The Lord Nelson
36 Trafalgar Street (01273) 695872
Start Time: 8.30pm
When: Every Tuesday
Cost: £1 per person
Team Size: maximum of 6
Prizes? 1st, 2nd and 3rd prizes are cash made from the quiz divided accordingly. A raffle is often held on the same night with usually a couple of bottles of red up for grabs. Ask Eddy about the gold stars….

The Greys
105 Southover Street (01273) 680734
Start Time: 8.00pm (Sharp!)
When: First Sunday of the month
Cost: £1 per person
Team Size: maximum of 6
Prizes? 1st prize takes the money. The booby prize, anything goes apparently. See what you can barter!

The Lion & Lobster
24 Sillwood Street (01273) 327229
Start Time: 8.30pm
When: Every Monday
Cost: £1 per person
Team Size: maximum of 6
Prizes? Cash prize.
General knowledge theme. An absolute hoot, but for masochists only; a zealous Chichester public school teacher leads proceedings with a beguiling mix of enthusiasm and befuddlement at the state of the world, setting questions ranging from up-to-date general knowledge to arcane academia. Make sure to be quiet whilst the quizmaster is talking!

The Fountainhead
102 North Road (01273) 628091
Start Time: 8.30pm
When: Every Sunday
Cost: £1 per person
Team Size: maximum of 6
Prizes? Cash prize

The Crescent
6 Clifton Hill (01273) 205260
Start Time: 8.30pm
When: Every Tuesday
Cost: £1 per person
Team Size: maximum of 6
Prizes? Cash prize.
A proper back street local with a pleasant garden if the quiz questions all get too much.

The Walmer Castle
95 Queens Park Road (01273) 682466
Start Time: 8.00pm
When: Every Monday
Cost: £1 per person
Team Size: maximum of 6
Prizes? Cash prize.
A weekly general knowledge quiz with a free prize raffle for unplaced teams.

Best Cocktails In Town...

Blanch House
17 Atlingworth Street, Brighton
(01273) 603504
Award winning cocktail bar located on the ground floor of a boutique hotel. Owner Chris Edwardes is former manager of The Groucho Club and can mix a mean cocktail, based on over 30 years experience.

Koba
135 Western Road, Brighton
(01273) 720059
Voted one of the Top Ten bars in the UK in 2005 by The Independent, this is a great place for a cocktail early or late. Happy hour is between 5 – 7pm in the public front bar all week. Live music on Thursdays and DJs at the weekend.

Pinxto People
95 Western Rd, Brighton
(01273) 732323
Upstairs at this lively tapas bar/restaurant you'll find a sophisticated comfortable bar area. Winner of the Observer Food Monthly Award for 'Best Place to Drink in the UK', they have an extensive and impressive range of cocktails, and you get free olives if you ask for them!

Bar Valentino
7a New Road, Brighton
(01273) 727898
Classy, chic and intimate.
Open 7pm – til late.

Neo
19 Oriental Place, Brighton
(01273) 711104
Situated in a stunning boutique hotel, the bar is open to non-residents and stays open at weekends until about 2am (closes earlier in the week). They mix an excellent cocktail and have a well stocked bar if you'd prefer a beer or a glass of wine.

Browns Bar
34 Ship Street, Brighton
(01273) 323501
This bar gets very noisy later on, but it's perfect for a pre-dinner aperitif or cocktail, and is right in the heart of town near lots of restaurants.

© Koba

© The Blanch House

Pub Crawls

Even if you live here you will never visit every pub this city has to offer; instead it is wiser to choose an area and get to know that well before moving on to the next. Here are some suggested routes:

Hove

Starting in Hove and heading into Brighton, **The Farm** on Farm Road is a good place to begin. Small and red, the sparkly lights will get you in the mood. Back on Western Road the **Duke of Norfolk** offers old school charm, especially on open mic night (with DJs at the weekend). Around the corner **The Robin Hood** looms, usually packed and noisy. Make some friends and take them with you. Hop across to Bedford Place where the **Lion & Lobster** may well greet you with a full Irish band. End the evening chilling at **The Hamptons** on Upper North Street where you can add your portrait to the visitor's wall to mark your accomplishment. And at the end of the road, oh look, there's a taxi rank!

North Laine

Handy for hopping off the train and straight into an ocean of calm is **The Evening Star** on Surrey Street. Sample some of the best beer Sussex has to offer before taking a deep breath and heading out into the famous North Laine. **The Earth and Stars** on Windsor Street offers organic drinks and eco-friendly ideals, with DJs at the weekend. From there down to Trafalgar Street and **The Lord Nelson** where friendly bar staff will tell you a story or two. You'll definitely meet some characters here. On to the lively New Road area and **The Mash Tun**. If it's a nice night, grab a table outside; if the queue for the bar is too long, pop next door to **Mrs Fitzherberts**. If you're still standing after all of this, round off the evening in **The Basketmakers** on Gloucester Road.

Hanover (Hangover?)

The sheer quantity (and quality) of pubs within yards of each other in Hanover can be daunting. And all of them on a great big hill. To ease into the upward bound crawl (don't worry, you come down again) start at **The London Unity** on Islingword Road for a stunning choice of beverages. The jukebox is free before 6pm, an incentive to start your crawl a little earlier. Carry on up to **The Constant Service** for a pint of Harveys (brewed locally in Lewes). Live bands and DJ's are often on offer with the legendary 'Stick It On' (your chance at the decks) on the 1st and 3rd Tuesday of the month. Then to the very top of Southover Street and **The Pub with No Name**. It's bright red, so you can't miss it - a proper local pub and always friendly. A downward stroll takes you to the **Charles Napier**, a friendly pub offering up Fullers beers, the occasional folk night and the trendiest ladies toilets in Hanover. And finally reaching **The Greys**, reward yourself with a well-deserved ale or guest Belgian beer and see who's playing live that night.

© Henry Law

04

Free Brighton & Hove

Brighton & Hove is often seen as an expensive city where you need money to have fun – but take heart, there's plenty to do for free…

No-cost entertainment options range from plentiful museums to beautiful walks in the surrounding area. The city is famous as a place where one can be entertained by just walking around or sitting on a bench, and watching the world go by ranks high in the local popularity stakes. In addition to the many free organised events throughout the year, there are buskers in the lanes, drummers on the beach, people practising poi on the Level… you can never be sure what you might run into.

This section lists some of the free attractions and events in the city, as well as some of the best walks and places to relax. As hard up locals know, Brighton & Hove can still be

The City's Top Free Activities

(as voted in The Deckchair Poll)

1. Walking Around
On a stroll around the centre, taking in the North Laine and the Lanes, you cannot help but be captivated by the cheeky joie de vivre that sings out at you from every shop and passing pedestrian. – Sheila

2. Swimming in the Sea
I love being able to walk to the sea for a dip, it's free, it's refreshing, more people should be doing it. I particularly like it out of season. – Max

3. The Beach and Walking on the Seafront

Cycling around Brighton © David Gray

4. People Watching
The people watching is first class. Why have organised parades when it's like that all year? – Peta

5. The Streets of Brighton

6. Pride
Brighton Pride enables everyone to enjoy a free day of diverse entertainment. – Local resident

7. Burning the Clocks
The burning of the clocks is inclusive and idiosyncratic and adventurous and is just what is needed on the shortest day of the year. – Mick

8. Museums

9. Open Houses in Brighton Festival
I love the Open House part of Brighton Festival, as you get the opportunity to meet loads of artists/potters etc and discuss their work with them. You can also have a good look round lots of houses and gardens in the area. – Jacqueline

10. Cycling
On my daily cycle along the seafront… I never cease to be astonished by the sea's different moods; every day is a treat. – Chris

Calendar of Events

Brighton has a calendar of established events, to which additions are often made. The dates may change from year to year, but full details can usually be found on the web, in the *Evening Argus* or one of the many free listings magazines in cafés and pubs around town.

March

Pioneer Motorcycle Run, Madeira Drive – Occurring on the third Sunday in March, this rally has run since the 1930s and is open to motorbikes made before 1915.

April

Brighton Coach Rally – Usually mid April. Mini and motorcycle runs may have more glamour, but bus drivers get their run to the seaside too. Check out the coach driver of the year obstacle challenge.

May

Mayday in Albion – A traditional Mayday celebration held in Queen's Park. Recent 'Mayday in Albion' celebrations featured maypole dancing, food stalls and folk music.

Pioneer Motorcycle Run © David Gray www.imagesbrighton.com

Children's Parade © Matthew Andrews

Children's Parade – The annual children's parade, organised by Same Sky, occurs on the first Saturday in May and is the opening event of Brighton Festival. Thousands of children take part, with samba bands leading the march through the town.

Brighton Festival – The Brighton Festival has been running since 1967. While most festival events require an entrance fee there are always free events held around the town, from small open-air performances to spectacular firework shows. With Brighton Festival Fringe growing in prominence in recent years there are now even more free activities throughout May. Full details can be found in the festival programmes and on their web sites www.brightonfestival.org and www.brightonfestivalfringe.org.uk.

Open Houses – The Open House programme runs throughout May. Started by Ned Hoskins in 1982, this annual event features local people who open their own homes as galleries to display work. This offers the chance to see some interesting and affordable art as well as more expensive pieces – guessing the price of items can be fun. Recent festivals have also seen experiments such as the Open Hotels.

Streets of Brighton – Founded by Zap Art in 1994, these free street events are part of Brighton Festival and occur in and around the North Laine. Due to lack of funding, events were radically scaled down this year and quite disappointing – so here's hoping funding is secured to return it to its former glory.

Naked Bike Ride © John Hazzard www.hazy.net

Brighton Hip-hop festival © David Gray

Streets of Brighton © Matthew Andrews

June

Chattri Memorial Service – Held on the third Sunday in June at the Chattri Memorial near Patcham. The half hour service takes place at 2:30pm.

Naked Bike Ride – A recent addition to the calendar, these bare-skinned pedallers aim to highlight the vulnerability of cyclists as well as the world's oil shortages. A colourful and rather raucous affair (and that's just the spectators), catch them around town at some point during the day.

July

Brighton Kite Festival – Held in Stanmer Park, this is a free kite festival with a relaxed atmosphere.

Brighton Hip-hop festival – The Brighton hip-hop festival features a range of events, some of which are free. Full details are released in the run-up to the festival.

August

Pride – Brighton's annual Pride parade and party is one of the highlights of the year and the largest free Pride event in the country. Pride started in 1992 as a small event on the Level and now over 100,000 people congregate for the grand finale in Preston Park. The day starts with a spectacular parade that makes its way from the seafront to the park, where a fairground and a number of dance stages are set up. Pride events run in the preceding week, as well as throughout the weekend. Pride is paid

Pride © David Gray www.imagesbrighton.com

Veteran Car Run © David Gray

for through donations at the events they run, so don't shirk the bucket when they pass it round.

November

Lewes Fireworks – Whilst definitely not in Brighton, many people make the journey to Lewes for the annual firework display. If the crowds and queues in Lewes seem too much, one can always find a hilltop and watch displays taking place across Brighton.

Veteran Car Run – Held on the first Sunday in November, pre-1905 vehicles make the journey from Hyde Park to London.

December

Burning the Clocks – This parade is usually held on the winter Solstice evening to light up the darkest day of winter, and involves a lantern procession followed by fires on the beach. The lanterns, made from willow canes and paper, take the form of clocks or symbolise time in imaginative ways. They are burned on the beach after their journey through town. Workshops related to the event take place around town in the run-up to the parade. An example costume can be seen in Brighton Museum.

Christmas Swim – On Christmas Day each year, members of Brighton Swimming Club gather for their Yuletide bathe - some wearing fancy dress. This happens at 11am close to the Palace Pier. Recent outings featured about 30 swimmers and many more spectators. The event has been running since the club was founded in 1860.

Bathing belles on The Palace Pier in 1936 © The Argus

The Seafront

Seafront Office

Seafront Office
141 King's Road Arches
Lower Esplanade
(01273) 292715
resort.services@brighton-hove.gov.uk

Dr. Richard Russell was instrumental in reviving the town's fortunes in the second half of the eighteenth century. It was the seafront that boosted the resort's early popularity, when his recommended 'seawater cure' became famous. Whether you're walking along the front, sitting on the pebbles, or listening to bands playing in the bars, summer in Brighton is unbeatable; and in winter, when most people stay away from the front, it can be even better – often you can get the whole beach to yourself.

The Palace (Brighton) Pier

I always wore my Sunday best when we went on the piers. Every summer they held a Bathing Belles Carnival competition on the Palace Pier.
Boxing Day Baby – Barbara Chapman (QueenSpark Books, 1994)

Entry to the Palace Pier is free, as is the use of their deckchairs. The pier provides good views of the town and, although you have to pay to use the rides, it is free to watch people screaming on some of the more outrageous ones. Horatio's bar can also throw up some highly entertaining moments, particularly when the stag and hen parties are in for the karaoke.

Kings Road Arches

Between the piers on the lower promenade lies the 'Artist's Quarter'. Originally the domain of fishermen, these studios now act as galleries displaying original paintings and artefacts at varying prices. Open all year round and well worth a look.

For a glimpse into the past – and the future – check out the clairvoyant Eva Petulengro ('50 years in Brighton!') and Professor Mirza, who has a list of 'hundreds of world famous personality endorsements' for his palm reading, of which Britt Ekland seems to be the only actual famous person.

Fishing Museum

For details of the city's seaside heritage, browse the old photos and exhibits at the Fishing Museum (see Museums and Galleries)

The West Pier

THEN

It's strange that I had never been on the West Pier before I applied for a vacancy, although I had lived in Hove for quite a few years. I thought it would be quite frightening working over the sea; strange thing was you never noticed it. Several times I saw porpoises basking in the sea. The first time I thought they were whales.
 Oh! What a Lovely Pier – Daphne Mitchell (QueenSpark Books, 1996)

AND NOW…
The West Pier stands with a sort of forlorn beauty, unable to believe its betrayal by the people of Brighton and Hove.
– Local resident

The ruined West Pier, destroyed by a series of fires, is one of the most remarkable sights, and a controversial landmark in the city. Locals see it either as an eyesore that should be pulled down or a ramshackle curiosity in elegant decline. Plans are well-advanced for the 'i360' West Pier Observation Tower and Heritage Centre: a 600 foot tower adjacent to the West Pier - rest assured this won't be free!

The nearby basketball court hosts rowdy pick-up games that are fast and furious, while the beach volleyball court often resembles a background scene from an episode of Baywatch. (Both are free but you must book the volleyball court by telephoning (01273) 725444. Not quite so frantic is petanque, for which there are two courts either side of the West Pier. *I'm pleased to see that playing petanque on the seafront terrains has become an established Brighton activity. Cool boules!* – Ray

The West Pier then … © The Royal Pavillion and Museums

… and now © Henry Law

The Level in 1970 © The Argus

Relaxing in The Pavilion Gardens © David Gray

Hove Lawns

The other side of the West Pier is Hove Lawns, which, in summertime, becomes a united nations of jumpers-for-goalposts football matches. And, of course, the sea always beckons for a paddle or a swim. Details of lifeguard patrols are displayed on signs around the beach.

The Beach After Dark

Barbecues are allowed on some areas of the seafront, after 6pm – check beach signs or the council website for up to date information. As night time develops, the area takes on a different flavour. Many beachside parties spring up in summer time, and around club chucking-out time the whole beach turns into a Glastonbury-like mélange of drunks, stoners, happy clubbers, and stag parties jumping naked into the sea.

Parks & Gardens

Brighton's parks are a credit to the city and I spend endless hours with my children in St. Anne's Well Gardens in particular. It has everything you need, a good café, a good playground, gardens, and a bowling green. – Vanessa

The Level, *Off Union Rd, Brighton*
In the early days of Brighton, the Level was a patch of swampy ground, which protected it from being developed. It was formally adopted by the town in 1822. In its time, it has been used for cricket matches, Mayday worker's rallies and large public dinners to celebrate coronations and the end of wars. Placed on a thin strip of land surrounded by roads, the Level is not a particularly rural park, but on summer evenings it can be magical with people practising juggling and poi, or just relaxing. There are often small games of football at the north end and there is a playground, a skate park and a cafe.

Stanmer Park, City outskirts,
near Sussex University
Stanmer Park is on the edge of Brighton. Lying next to the university, the park contains the small village of Stanmer, which has a beautiful church and a tearoom. The park also contains the largest area of woodland in Brighton. The grounds at the back of Stanmer House are known as 'The Pleasureground'. Amongst the grand old trees you may stumble upon one which fell in the 1987 storm and has been carved to resemble a group of badgers by local sculptor Reece Ingram.

Pavilion Gardens, City centre, Brighton
On the edge of the North Laine area, the grounds of the Royal Pavilion provides a pleasant environment for lunching office-workers, visitors and sun seeking locals. Deckchairs are available and there are often buskers, some rather better than others. Pavilion Gardens Café (see Eating Section, p.59) serves delicious homemade cakes and sandwiches, and a variety of teas.

Queen's Park, Between Hanover and Kemptown, Brighton
Queen's Park started out as a pleasure garden in 1836 and was named after Queen Adelaide. It became a public park in 1891. Set within a small valley, the park features a wildlife garden and a duck pond. At the start of May the park hosts the annual 'Mayday in Albion' celebrations.

Preston Park, Off London Rd, Brighton
The town's first public park, Preston Park was opened in 1883. It is the largest park area in Brighton with places to play bowls and football, as well as a playground and a cycle track (with racing on Wednesday evenings). The rotunda cafe sits within the recently renovated rose gardens.

On the opposite side of the main road is the Rockery (also known as the Rookery after the small wood that was once there), which is a hillside garden with some excellent views. It is believed locally that the Rockery's design was based on the Chinese 'Willow' pattern.

At the north end of the park is Preston Manor. In the grounds of this house is a small pets' cemetery. All its permanent guests were formerly owned by council employees. The walled garden is secluded and peaceful and there is also a small church featuring old murals.

St. Anne's Well Gardens,
Somerhill Road, Hove
In 1750 Dr Richard Russell erected a basin at St Anne's Well expounding the beneficial properties of its waters. Laid out as a pleasure garden in 1850 by Sir Isaac Goldsmid, it was later acquired by Hove Council and became a public park in 1908.

St. Nicholas Church and Churchyard,
Dyke Rd, Brighton (01273) 321399
A short distance from the Clock Tower and Churchill Square is St. Nicholas Church, the oldest church in Brighton. The grounds of the church feature

memorials for many of the town's famous residents, such as Phoebe Hessel and Martha Gunn. (See **Literary Walk**) The churchyard across the road provides a quiet place away from the bustle of the town.

Extra Mural Cemetery,
Lewes Road, Brighton
Visiting a cemetery for a day out might seem strange, but it was a popular activity in Victorian times. The Extra-Mural cemetery, just off Lewes Road, is a stunning place to spend an afternoon. It is set in 70 acres of land and the first burial occurred in 1851. A number of Brighton's famous residents are buried here. There are some impressive memorials, like the 15 ton memorial for John Urpeth Rastrick, founder of London, Brighton & South Coast Railways, which was placed so it would be visible from the station. There is also a memorial for Edward Bransfield (1795-1852), the first person known to have seen Antarctica. The city's Bear Road and Woodvale Cemeteries are adjacent to the Extra-Mural Cemetery and also provide peaceful respite from the bustle of the city centre.

St. Bartholomew's Church, Ann St. (off London Rd), Brighton (01273) 620491
St. Bartholomew's church is 4 feet higher than Westminster Abbey and local legend claims (inaccurately apparently) that its proportions match those of Noah's Ark. It's said to be the tallest one-storey building in Europe, and is sometimes open to visitors. Well worth a look.

Museums & Galleries

The city has a number of museums and galleries, and it seems that every café in town is selling artwork - some wonderful, some less so. Listing every gallery in the town would be difficult, but many can be easily found in a stroll around the Lanes and North Laine area. Below are some of particular interest.

Booth Museum, 194 Dyke Rd, Brighton (01273) 292777
The Booth Museum of Natural History is open almost every day of the year and contains a collection based around taxidermy exhibits gathered by Thomas Booth, who built the gallery in 1874. When Booth died the Natural History Museum declined the collection due to lack of space so it was given to the town on condition that the displays not be altered. The main hall of the museum features displays of stuffed birds. The museum also features a display of skeletons (including a dodo), collections of butterflies, and a toad stone.

Brighton Museum, 4-5 Pavilion Buildings, Brighton (01273) 290900
Renovated in the last few years, Brighton Museum has an eclectic theme and a variety of exhibits on show. The costume collection features interactive displays showing outfits worn by different Brighton sub-cultures. There is a collection of 'World Art', and a number of exhibitions dedicated to the city of Brighton. There is also a furniture

Art on show at Brighton Museum in 1947

(and left) © Royal Pavilion and Museums, Brighton & Hove

exhibition and the 700-piece collection, Mr. Willett's Popular Pottery, featuring pieces made between 1600 and 1900. It houses a stylish café which serves high quality refreshments.

Fabrica, 40 Duke St, Brighton (01273) 778646
The Fabrica Gallery opened in 1996 and occupies the old Holy Trinity Church, built in 1817. Fabrica commissions art installations specific to the unique space.

Fishing Museum, 210 Kings Road Arches, Brighton (01273) 723064
The fishing museum can be found tucked under the promenade between the two piers, and offers an interesting historical perspective on the town's fishing heritage.

Graffiti
Brighton has some fantastic graffiti. Places worth checking are Black Rock (on the seafront, towards the Marina), the North Laine (particularly Kensington Street) and the outside of the Gladstone pub out on the Lewes Road, which has two works by Banksy.

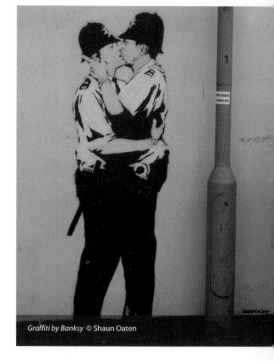

Graffiti by Banksy © Shaun Oaten

Hove Museum, 19 New Church Road, Hove (01273) 290200
This museum features displays devoted to film, paintings, toys and local history. There is a small cinema showing fascinating free films from the early days of cinema, when Hove was home to a number of pioneering filmmakers.

The Permanent Gallery and Bookstore,
20 Bedford Place, Brighton
07979 602291
www.permanentgallery.com
The Permanent Gallery is situated in a
side street off Western Road. It has regular
exhibitions and also holds frequent live
events, such as talks from exhibiting
artists and spoken word evenings.

North Laine Photography,
7-8 Kensington Gardens, Brighton
(01273) 628794
www.northlainephotography.co.uk
The North Laine Photography Gallery is
on the first floor of Snooper's Paradise.
While this is a commercial gallery (with a
number of classic Brighton images for
sale), it often hosts shows and
exhibitions of local photographs. North
Laine Photography also organise an
annual open photography show.

Mechanical Memories, 250c Kings Rd
Arches, Brighton (01273) 608620
www.sussexmuseums.co.uk
This museum is devoted to old-
fashioned arcade games and
entertainment. Visitors need to buy old
pennies to play the machines.

Libraries

Jubilee Library Jubilee Street, Brighton
(01273) 290800 www.citylibraries.info
This recently built landmark building has
already won several national awards for
its innovative eco-friendly design. It hosts
many free activities. Phone for details
and opening times.

Hove Library,
182-186 Church Road, Hove
(01273) 296937 www.citylibraries.info
Recently refurbished Hove library offers
free internet access and a wide range of
other services.
(See www.citylibraries.info for full list of
branch libraries)

Free Internet
Lots of cafes and bars now offer 'free'
internet access. However, a team of
community volunteers has set up
www.piertopier.net that allows you to
surf for free without even having to buy
a cup of coffee. So, next time you're
clubbing down on the seafront, you'll
have an excuse to bring your laptop.
Equipment and weather permitting, you
can connect anywhere from the West
Pier to the last groyne before the Palace
Pier, and connection works best if you
are in sight of the beach nodes - which
are at Riptide, the Sailing Club, and the
Fishing Museum.

24 Hour Museum
www.24hourmuseum.org.uk
A great website that where you can
discover lots of free events and
exhibitions. Just type in Brighton and
wait for the listings…

Heritage Open Days
www.heritageopendays.org.uk
Every year on four days in September,
buildings that are normally closed to the
public open their doors. Check out the
website to discover which of Brighton
& Hove's buildings will be taking part.

Under Brighton's Victorian brick viaduct © Beatrice Haverich www.beatricehaverich.com

Walks

As you walk under the majestic Victorian brick viaduct… hearing the trains belch and rumble above … no matter what time of day, it's like someone turned off the fancy lights of Brighton. In a city dominated by architecture coated in fondant icing, the dankness of this particular spot renders it (momentarily) dirty, fetid and pulsing with a darker life-force. And as the city continues apace towards its laminate-floored, glass-fronted future, this bit of New England Road is a necessary reminder of a too-easily forgotten past. – Matt

The City's Favourite Journeys/Walks

(as voted in The Deckchair Poll)

1. Undercliffe Walk – Brighton to Rottingdean

In times gone by Rottingdean had a lovely sandy beach until in the 1930s when the undercliff walk was built from Brighton to Saltdean and the huge concrete groynes took the place of the lovely old wooden groynes. Since then nearly all our sand has disappeared. – Margaret Ward – Memories of Rottingdean

2. Walking along the seafront

3. North Laine

4. Stanmer Park

5. Bus to Devil's Dyke

6. Bus to Ditchling Beacon

7. Bus to Cuckmere Haven

8. Volks Railway

Riding or driving on Volk's was part of my childhood. I love railways and, like most little boys, I always wanted to drive a train. Now, in retirement, I have achieved that ambition. This railway, even in its much altered present form, takes me back to those sunny days in the 1930s. – Peter

The Volks Railway in the 1930s © Royal Pavilion and Museums, Brighton & Hove

Deckchair Guided Walks

A Stroll Through Hove's Pink Past...

Start the walk with an ice cream or a coffee at Marrocco's on Hove seafront. It is situated near the King Alfred Leisure Centre (see Cafés and Tea Shops in the Eating Section).Then cross the busy main road to the south end of St Aubyns. **Virginia Woolfe** spent several summers at 9 St Aubyns as a child, although there is no blue plaque here to mark this. Turn left out of St Aubyns heading east along Kingsway and turn left into Fourth Avenue. Following Oscar Wilde's self-imposed exile from Britain, **Lord Alfred Douglas** married and had a son. The marriage didn't work out and in 1925 he moved with his mother to 35 Fourth Avenue. During their relationship he and Oscar had made several trips to the Brighton area, Wilde wrote The Importance of Being Earnest in nearby Worthing. Continue to the top of the avenue and turn right into Western Road, cross over and turn left into The Drive. A blue plaque at 20 The Drive, a turreted gothic building, commemorates novelist **Ivy Compton-Burnett** who lived here. The writer's family moved to Hove when Ivy was a child as her father, a successful vegetarian homeopathic doctor, believed the sea air would be beneficial to the health of his thirteen children. Ivy stayed in Hove until she was thirty, when she left for London. She subsequently met her partner, the writer and antiquarian Margaret Jourdain with whom she lived until Margaret's death

The Royal Albion Hotel in 1900 © Royal Pavilion and Museums

in 1951. Return to Western Road, heading east again. Cross over and turn right into First Avenue. 30 First Avenue was home to the Compton-Burnett family when they first relocated to Hove. This very grand street with a couple of mews at the top and yellow stoned houses with wrought iron balconies leads you back down to the sea. Not strictly pink, but worth a mention, 12 First Avenue was the childhood home of novelist **Patrick Hamilton** (author of the homoerotic play Rope). Turn left out of First Avenue onto Kingsway for a breath of sea air taking in the Regency facades along the front. Turn left into Brunswick Square which is a veritable sea of blue plaques. The one you are looking for is at number 45 Brunswick Square, birthplace of **Edward Carpenter**: socialist, critic, writer, poet, thinker, vegetarian and mystic! His writings made an important contribution to the development of the English socialist movement and his radical lifestyle was a refreshing contrast to the oppressive middle class values of late Victorian England, and still inspires many today. Walk round the square and continue along the seafront to the Royal Albion Hotel, reputedly Oscar Wilde's favourite Brighton hotel. Alternatively you can nip along Western Road and finish your walk with afternoon tea at Tallula's Tea Rooms behind Waitrose (see Cafés and Tea Rooms in the Eating Section).

A Literary Walk From Port Hall to the heart of the city

Featuring writers and those who have been written about…

There is a plaque to commemorate the birthplace of **Eric Gill (1882 - 1940)** at 31 Hamilton Road, Brighton, (just off the Old Shoreham Road, near Seven Dials). The son of a local curate, Gill was a talented artist, stone carver, typeface designer and sculptor (Gill carved the inscription on Oscar Wilde's tomb in Paris.) Fond of erotic imagery, Gill was also sexually adventurous, and his diaries detail his amorous liaisons, which include some same sex experiences. He married Ethel Moore in 1904 and moved to nearby Ditchling in 1907, where he became the centre of an artist's community. Leaving Hamilton Road, head south via York Grove and Howard Place to Buckingham Road.

31 Buckingham Road is the birthplace of Victorian illustrator **Aubrey Beardsley (1872 - 1898)**. A complex character, he like Gill, was fond of affairs with both sexes. Beardsley illustrated Oscar Wilde's play Salome and his distinctive style became associated with Wilde. In fact this association was to prove problematic for Beardsley following Wilde's imprisonment for sexual offences, eventually leading to his dismissal as art editor of the literary journal The Yellow Book. At the end of Buckingham Road turn left and head towards the oldest building in Brighton: **St Nicholas' Church.**

…*The church survived a raid by French pirates, who burnt the mediaeval town of Brighthelmstone in 1533.*

Why was it built on a hill? To avoid coastal erosion? To be protected from French pirates? Probably so that a fire lit on the big flat church tower could provide a beacon for fishermen.

There are spectacular views from the churchyard. You're standing on the spine of a ridge here. Lower down, the old town grew up on a defendable site by a stream.
– Geoffrey Mead
(www.mybrightonandhove.org.uk)

Several notorious Brightonians are buried in the church yard here: one being vocalist **Anna Maria Crouch (1763 -1805)**. As well as being known as a singer and actress she is also famous for a brief liaison with the Prince of Wales. There is a portrait of Anna Maria by Edward Harding in the National Portrait Gallery. She died suddenly in Brighton on 2 October 1805 and conflicting reports state the cause of death as either a carriage accident or heavy drinking!

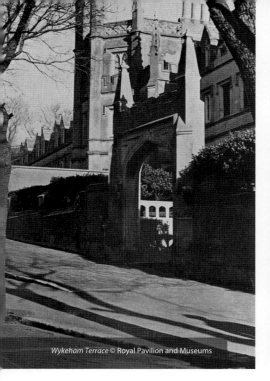

Wykeham Terrace © Royal Pavilion and Museums

Martha Gunn © Royal Pavilion and Museums

Martha Gunn (1776 - 1815) was a famous 'dipper': the person who would stand in the sea by the steps of the bathing machine and dip the bather in the sea. She and Phoebe Hessel (1713 – 1821) are also buried here. If living to 107 isn't note worthy enough, Phoebe is also alleged to have dressed as a soldier and served in the West Indies in order to be near her lover Samuel Golding. Just below the church yard is Wykeham Terrace where British character actress Dame Flora Robson (1902 – 1984) and her two sisters lived for many years (at number 7). Sir Roy Strong also lived here at No. 8, before moving to his current house in Herefordshire.

Wykeham is a gothic inspired terrace, an oasis of calm set behind a thick stone wall, sheltering from the city.

Wykeham Terrace, built between 1822 and 1830, has been home to soldiers, squatters and even former prostitutes, although it now seems far more genteel. Number 1 Wykeham Terrace has apparently housed not one but two 1960s pop stars: Leo Sayer and Adam Faith both occupied the property in the past. The houses on the western side of the terrace are numbered from 7-12, with a 7a next to no.7. It was considered unlucky to have a number 13 in the row! – Claire Andrews (www.mybrightonandhove.org.uk)

Leave St Nicholas' and head down North Street. Halfway down on the left is the Premier Lodge Hotel. This is the former site of 9 Mulberry Square, North Street, long since demolished, and once home to vocalist Anna Maria Crouch (see

WE WOULD BE
PLEASED TO TAKE
YOUR ORDER
FOR INTERVAL
DRINKS

The Colonnade Bar © David Gray www.imagesbrighton.com

above). Turning right into Ship Street, follow the road round to the left until you come to 58 Ship Street, currently ASK pizza restaurant. Writer **Clementina Black (1853 - 1922)** was born here. Clementina's first novel A Sussex Idyll was published in 1877.

Just round the corner is Friends Meeting House The peaceful walled garden contains an early 19th Century Quaker Meeting House. Its foundations were built in 1804-5 on land that was owned by local Quaker John Glaisyer.

Following the road round to the left you will come upon Meeting House Lane (one of the entrances to The Lanes). Feed your way through The Lanes and back out into North Street. Cross the road and over on the left is New Road which houses the historic Theatre Royal. Actress and writer **Mary Elizabeth Braddon (1835 - 1915)** lived in Brighton from 1857- 1860 appearing at The Theatre Royal under the stage name Mary Seyton and writing as a journalist for the Brighton Herald . She lodged at both 26 and 34 New Road, Brighton. In 1860 she gave up the stage and became very rich writing sensational fiction; she had great success with her best seller Lady Audley's Secret (1862) which is still in print (Oxford World's Classics) and was adapted for television in 2000. **The**

The Colonnade Bar (see Drinking section) next to the Theatre Royal is worth a peek or a stop for refreshments. Re-enter North Road and continue down to East Street on the right. Martha Gunn (see above) lived at 34 East Street. A little way down on the left is Steine Lane, a passage way at the end of which is 54 The Steine (currently the YMCA). This villa was given as a gift to **Mrs Fitzherbert (1754 - 1823)** by her lover The Prince Regent. Although the Prince had many subsequent mistresses, on his deathbed in 1823, the then Monarch, King George IV is reputed to have had a miniature of his first love around his neck. Maria Fitzherbert's villa was sold to the YMCA in 1884. Turn right onto the Steine and head for the nearby **Mock Turtle Café** (see Cafés and Tearooms in the Eating Section) where the walk ends.

Kemptown Notorieties Walk

Sussex Square

The walk starts in historic Sussex Square. The building of the square commenced in 1823 and the facades were complete by 1827. Both Sussex Square and adjoining Lewes Crescent have had their fair share of distinguished residents and visitors. Lewis Carroll (Reverend Charles Dodgson) spent summers at no. **No. 11,** between 1874 and 1887 and Elenor Marx (daughter of Karl) taught at **No. 29,** which was once Miss Hall's School. Vita Sackville West sought sanctuary at **No. 39 - 40**, the home of her mother, Lady Sackville during the scandal surrounding her affair with Violet Trefusis in 1919. Lady Sackville bought 39 - 40 Sussex Square (which are now flats) in 1918. In 1923, when Lady Sackville moved to White Lodge at Black Rock, Brighton: a seven day sale was required to clear the Sussex Square house. Amongst the treasures on offer there were sculptures

Lewes Crescent © David Gray www.imagesbrighton.com

by Rodin and Epstein and a 42 stone diamond necklace. Antony Dale, author, historian and conservationist, lived at **No. 46** between 1914 and 1962.

Lewes Crescent

The Sixth Duke of Devonshire (after whom Duke's Mound is named) lived at **No. 1** (which is now Fife House). Lord Elwyn Jones (Labour Lord Chancellor) and his wife, Polly Binder (artist and writer), lived at **No. 17** from 1966-1989. Dame Anna Neagle was a former resident of **No. 18** and lived here with her film producer husband, Herbert Wilcox from 1953-1969. Jack Buchanan (actor/manager impresario) lived at **No. 19,** and the Lawrence Sisters, founders

of Roedean school, lived at **No. 25**. Leaving the crescent head west back towards Brighton along Marine Parade. After about 10 minutes you'll arrive at Burlington Street on the right. Comedian Max Miller lived at **25 Burlington Street** for fifteen years during the height of his fame. There is a blue plaque here to commemorate Brighton's 'Cheeky Chappie'. Local legend has it that when Max was performing in London, it would be written into his contract that he could appear second to last on the bill so he could hot foot it over to Victoria to be on the 11pm Brighton Belle back to his beloved Brighton. Former railway staff have reported that the train would wait for Max to arrive at Victoria before it left!

Heading back to Marine Parade, just along from Burlington Street a plaque outside **4 Royal Crescent**, commemorates its most famous resident: Laurence Olivier, who lived here with his wife Joan Plowright until the 1970s. A regular on the Brighton Belle express train to London, in 1972 Lord Olivier won his battle to keep kippers on the train's breakfast menu; sadly though, the train itself was axed later that year.

Just along from Royal Crescent at **79 Marine Parade** is **Bedford House,** once home to playwright **Sir Terence Rattigan (1911 - 1977)** who bought the property in 1961. He is perhaps best remembered for his plays: *The Browning Version*, *French Without Tears* and *The Winslow Boy*. Rattigan also penned the film script for Graham Greene's *Brighton Rock*. His work often dealt with complicated relationships and this may have had something to do with the fact that he was gay. Although after the war his style became a little out dated, Rattigan had a keen eye and was an early champion of playwright, Joe Orton, investing £3,000 in the 1964 production of Orton's *Entertaining Mr Sloane*.

Just further down the road at **Lanes Hotel, (70 - 72 Marine Parade)** a plaque, celebrates the stay of one of its most famous visitors: **Ivor Novello (1893 - 1951)**. David Ivor Davies became a household name in 1914 with his popular First World War song, *Keep The Home Fires Burning*. A fine soprano and songwriter, as an actor he was hailed as the new Valentino. He met his lover, actor Bobbie Andrews in 1917 and they

One of Brighton's many blue plaques © Helen Fitzgerald

were together for 35 years. Novello is said to have written his successful 1935 show *Glamorous Nights* whilst staying at Lanes Hotel.

Still on Marine Parade, just past Lower Rock Gardens and the New Steine is Wentworth Street. Successful journalist Nancy Spain (1917 - 1964) rented **10 Wentworth Street** in 1957 when she came to Brighton to start work on a new book. Nancy was also a novelist of humorous fiction as well as being a well known radio and TV personality and regularly appeared on *Juke Box Jury*. It was in Brighton that she met the publisher Joan Werner Laurie (1920 - 1964) who became her life partner. Sadly Joan and Nancy died in a plane crash in 1964 at the height of Nancy's fame.

Double back on yourself and head for some superb snacks and drinks at bar/restaurant **Brighton Rocks** in Rock Place (see Best Sunday Roasts, p.79 in the Drinking Section).

05

Shopping in Brighton & Hove

The era of the bland homogenous High Street may well be upon us with the same shops in identical looking town centres throughout the land. However Brighton & Hove still manages to offer some great independent shopping. As the city evolves around them, we feature a selection of retailers who are standing the test of time.

The City's Top Ten Shops

(as voted in The Deckchair Poll)

1. Infinity Foods
Good prices, local produce and no excess packaging. – Local resident
(see page 116)

2. Taj
The atmosphere and the music in the Taj is great. It is more like going on holiday rather than shopping. – Philip
(see page 118)

3. Snoopers Paradise
(see page 126)

© Blackout

4. City Books and Kemp Town Books
Kemp Town Books is terrific. Though small it has an imaginative, intelligent selection of books for real book lovers. They support local writers and they host writing workshops for the community. – Alison

5. Blackout
Quirky, chic and colourful! – Deb
(see page 114)

6. Dockerills
(see page 132)

7. Resident Records
Resident is one of the friendliest record shops I've been to. The people who work there are always approachable and helpful and seem excited about music without being snobbish about different tastes. – Cora
(see page 125)

8. Rounder Records
Rounder - a financial black hole with my name on it. – Ian
(see page 125)

9. The Record Album
...Wonderfully enthusiastic, knowledgeable owner, with a collection to make a record buyer cry. His window display of the soundtracks to the films currently broadcast is astounding.
– Local resident
(see page 124)

10. Velvet
(see page 115)

Shopping Areas

*'The 1875 directory for East Brighton
listed 35 bootmakers, 3 breweries,
19 dressmakers, 15 tailors, 2 watchmakers,
2 tinners, 2 brushmakers and
2 basketmakers. By 1974 they had
virtually all disappeared…'*
Shops Book – Neil Griffiths
(QueenSpark Books, 1978)

In addition to its central shopping areas,
Brighton & Hove boasts several thriving
local retail communities which offer a
glimpse into the city's past. If you have
time to explore, it is well worth making
the detour to Kemp Town and Seven
Dials or taking a bus further out to
somewhere like Old Portslade where the
Emmaus community is situated (see
Charity Shops on page 128).

North Laine

Situated north of 'The Lanes', but not
'related', the North Laine has a uniqueness
that manages to encapsulate Brighton, for
good or ill. The name comes from the old
term 'Laine' meaning an open field, but
the area started to become built up
around 1780. Along its main
thoroughfares and side streets you'll find
shops selling comics, retro and ultra-
modern clothes, wholefoods, sex aids, a
gamut of the-latest-fad juice bars,
vegetarian shoes (go in and ask them…)
furniture, fudge, beer, many types of
coffee, and plenty of tarot, 'aura photos'
and other new age flim-flammery.

Western Road in Edwardian times © Royal Pavilion and Museums, Brighton & Hove

Kensingron Gardens © David Gray

The Lanes © David Gray www.imagesbrighton.com

The Lanes

Following a broadly medieval street pattern (even though the original buildings were destroyed by the French in 1519), the maze-like Lanes offer a convincing olde worlde shopping experience. There is a big focus on jewellery, although this can often mean the passageways are barred by couples buying for their nuptials. If peering at lots of shiny things takes its toll, stop off in the homely Bath Arms on Union Street for some pub grub and a decent pint. Newer additions to the Lanes' culinary sights, smells and tastes, are the well-regarded champagne and oyster bar **Riddle & Finns** on Meeting House Lane - and the bustling, family-run **Casa Don Carlos** in Union Street (see the Eating Section).

Hove

Whilst not being as focused a shopping experience as parts of Brighton, Hove does, nevertheless, have reasons for enticing you to wander. The shopping area is centred around George Street, a pleasant pedestrianised area bordered by Blatchington Road to the north and Church Road to the south. Church Road itself appears at first glance to be a fairly standard main street, however on closer inspection some real treats reveal themselves. Chief amongst these is the wondrous **Burkitts** (see page 130). Blatchington Road (at the end of George Street) is largely for DIY and charity shop enthusiasts, but has also found room for Hove's only sex shop, **Ignition** at No.8, which opened in 2003 to general local approval.

Church Road, Hove © JJ Waller

Kemp Town

Not the first area one thinks of when planning a shopping trip, but there are a few gems. The area is worth a visit anyway, just for the vibe of the neighbourhood which is bound up with its status as the Gay Capital of the UK. 'Camptown' – an old gag – conjures up images of feather boas and disco music, but that's only a slice of Kemp Town; the area has an edginess, earthiness, and occasional shabbiness, which defies easy definition, and its shops reflect its real diversity.

Seven Dials

Whilst not known for its shopping, Seven Dials has a few shops worth a visit. The main shopping street is Dyke Road which crosses the mini roundabout.

And when you've done the shops, this is a nice place to sit for a while and watch irate drivers try to bully their way through and around the seven junctions that gives the neighbourhood its name.

Gift Shops

Appendage,

36 Kensington Gardens, Brighton
(01273) 605901
Hilary Ormisher has owned Appendage for over 18 years. Both a gallery and a shop selling work by Brighton makers and British designers, Appendage sells jewellery, textiles, ceramics, mosaic, glass hangings and much more. Their window displays are always striking and you'll be sure to find a unique gift to take home.

© Blackout

Blackout, 53 Kensington Place, Brighton
(01273) 671741
Tucked away in Kensington Place,
Blackout smells as good as it looks.
Its enticing perfume lures you in and, if
that doesn't work, maybe Brian's charms
will do the trick (he's one of the shop's
cats). Selling kitsch accessories and
things for the house as well as fashion,
jewellery and cards, this is a perfect shop
to browse.

Cissy Mo, 38 Sydney St/ 88 Western Rd,
Brighton (01273) 607777/202008
www.cissymo.co.uk
The last word in kitsch, residents
obviously like this hall of fun because
there are now two shops in the city.
Cissy Mo's wares include pink washing-
up gloves trimmed with leopard print,
telephones in the shape of big red
plastic lips, glow-in-the-dark rubber
ducks, and smoking stickers saying
'Smoking Makes You Look Sexy',
'I could get hit by a bus tomorrow' and
'Nobody Likes a Quitter'! Cissy Mo also
sponsors a room at the Hotel Pelirocco

© The Lavender Room

in Hove called Cissy Mo's Magic Garden
where the ceiling is covered in plastic
green lawn.

The Lavender Room, 16 Bond Street,
Brighton (01273) 220380
www.lavender-room.co.uk
A slice of luxury, The Lavender Room
stands out in the North Laine for its
minimal white and pastel window

to this end it sells pieces of antique furniture, gorgeous clothing, Moroccan bowls, handpainted tealights, vintage cushions and quilts, all wrapped in lavender tissue paper and ribbon. The owners travel far and wide to purchase things that are both different and exotic. Check the website and the handy 'Send an e-Hint' facility - there's nothing like getting what you want.

Pussy, 3a Kensington Gardens/ 3 Bartholomews, Brighton (01273) 604861/749852 www.pussyhomeboutique.co.uk Winners of independent retailer of the year 2005, this shop is a true original. Calling itself a 'home boutique' the store stocks everything from retro home décor to Hello Kitty vibrators. Also famous for selling Britney some saucy badges, just as she embarked on her downward spiral…

Velvet, 27+ 29 Bond St, Brighton/ 10 George St, Hove (01273) 326007 www.velvet.co.uk This shop is unashamedly girlie, and will appeal to anyone (male or female) who has ever wished for their own boudoir. The shops are extremely attractive from the outside, making full use of the bow windows and giving the North Laine a glamorous 'lift' with a touch of 'Ooh la la!'. Shoes with bows, brightly striped neckties, satin cushions, girlie handbags, it's all here. One of the shops in Bond Street also sells furniture. This is the place to buy a gift for the woman who's already bought everything.

displays, which exude stylish chic. The type of woman who shops here probably never raises her voice and always wears silk lingerie, but that won't stop the rest of us gaining entry. Once through the doors you'll find yourself transported to a land of elegance. Beautiful materials abound: silk, satin, cotton, shell, mirror and lots more. Its aim is to be a one-stop lifestyle shop and

Specialist Food Shops

'The first thing you saw when you went into Harry Gardner's greengrocers* shop was a little notice. It was propped up on the counter facing the door so that you couldn't miss it- not much more than a ticket really - dark green with posh gold letters and it read:
PLEASE DO NOT ASK FOR CREDIT'
Our Small Corner – Sid Manville
(QueenSpark Books 1994)

(* Harry Gardner's greengrocers was in Bear Road)

Sweets galore at Caramella © Helen Fitzgerald

Audrey's Chocolates, 28 Holland Road, Hove/16 Regent Arcade, Brighton (01273) 735561
www.audreyschocolates.co.uk
An Honorary Member of the Guild of Master Craftsmen (do they have Master Craftswomen?) this shop has created bespoke chocolates for over 40 years. On its own in a residential street, but well worth the visit, Audrey's is a paragon of fine service and quality product.

Caramella, 29a Kensington Gardens, Brighton (01273) 570118
www.caramella.co.uk
Flying saucers, love hearts, giant gobstoppers, sherbet dabs, 20 types of Dutch liquorice, parma violets (uurrggh) and even a good selection of sugar free sweets (eh?). There is probably not a sweet invented that doesn't feature in their 'pic- n-mix' selection (knocks Woolworth's into a cocked hat for variety and cost), and there is also a good selection of fudges and toffees.

Infinity Foods, 25 North Road, Brighton (01273) 603563
Infinity Foods Café, 50 Gardner St, Brighton (01273) 670743
www.infinityfoods.co.uk
Infinity Foods is committed to the highest of ethical and environmental standards, aiming to allow no GMOs in its chain. Audited annually by The Soil Association, Infinity actively promotes fair trade and is a founder member of Genetic Food Alert. The retail side of the business was set up in 1970 and became

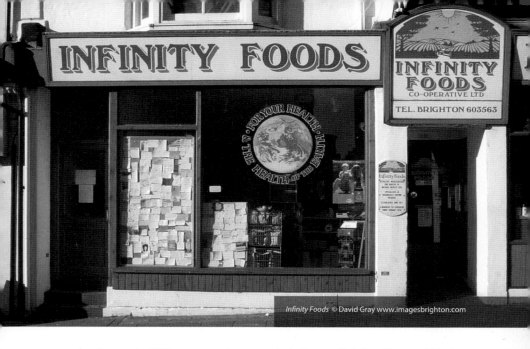

Infinity Foods © David Gray www.imagesbrighton.com

a workers' co-op in 1979, now carrying over 1,500 organic lines. Even on a wintry afternoon midweek the place is teeming with shoppers. This place feeds the spirit of Brighton and has a large following inside and outside the city. There is also an Infinity Foods vegetarian cafe in Gardner Street catering for many special diets, so it's just a hop, skip and a jump to test out their produce.

The Real Patisserie, Two shops
43 Trafalgar St, Brighton (01273) 570719
25 Western Rd, Brighton (01273) 711110
www.realpatisserie.co.uk
Open since 1997, The Real Patisserie is a delightful bakers specializing in traditional French bread and cakes, all made on the premises. Located just down from the station (and at Western Road in Hove), famous customers have included Cate Blanchett, Eddie Izzard,

Judy Cornwell, Julian Clary and Mark Williams. The owner admits that people thought they were mad to set up the original shop on Trafalgar Street which was, at that time, very run-down. But Real Patisserie has stolen a march on the Doubting Thomases because the area has now been stylishly regenerated. The shop is brightly painted with white and pink décor and its shelves groan under the weight of piles of gleaming goodies (it's that French glaze) and home-made fudge. Speciality breads include campaillou, dark, thick-crusted and slightly soured. There is also something called 'spelt', made with 'wheat's natural ancestor' and low in gluten too (it was used for bread-making in Roman times). They have a wholesale arm to the business, and also provide outside catering supplying savouries, pastries, petits fours, pizzas and quiches.

Exciting flavours at Taj © Helen Fitzgerald

Sussex in the City, 12c Meeting House Lane, Brighton (01273) 7477679
www.sussexandthecity.co.uk
A new kid on the block, Sussex in the City which opened in May 2006 has already won Best Sussex Food Shop 2006/7 at the Sussex Food Awards. The shop prides itself on stocking the best locally sourced Sussex produce and guarantees that all its wares come from no more than 50 miles away. So if it's a bottle of organic perry you're after, or maybe a jar of Sussex made lemon curd, be sure to pop in here first.

Taj, Three shops
95 Western Road/13-15 St James's St, Brighton (01273) 325027
21 Bedford Pl, Brighton (01273) 325126
Taj Natural Foods has just opened its latest store at the bottom of St James's Street. With its wealth of produce, this Asian inspired food store is going head to head with some of the city's supermarkets in its bid to poach their organic customers. As well as supporting local Sussex suppliers, the store's ethnic range of products encompasses vegetarian, vegan, and special diets. The original store in Bedford Place has been there for over 25 years, with the upstairs used as a mosque until larger premises were found nearby.

Yum Yum, 22-23 Sydney Street, Brighton (01273) 606777
A Chinese supermarket with an upstairs noodle bar (E-Kagen), offering a wide range of products from tinned squid, cooking sauces, fresh herbs and vegetables to tea sets and woks.

Bramptons Kemp Town, 114 St George's Road, Brighton (01273) 682611
For over 22 years Brighton born proprietor, Paul Williams, has provided excellent customer service and quality meats. The shop is a specialist stockist of South Downs lamb and also operates a quality cheese shop next door. Bramptons was the winner of the prestigious Sussex Butcher of the Year Award 2006/7.

Archers, 128 Islingword Rd, Brighton (01273) 603234
Archers Organic Butchers and Game Dealers has been a family business since 1936. It is the city's only organic butchers.

Arkwrights, 86 Beaconsfield Road, Brighton (01273) 552740
Natasha Stevenson and Ivan Pew have owned and run this well-stocked deli for five years. They also cook lots of delicious food to take away - now that's what we call handy!

Canhams, 48 Church Road, Hove (01273) 731021
Canhams the butchers stock a fine array of locally-sourced meats, pies – the fruit ones in the window are worth the trip alone - and cheeses, and people, including local DJ Fatboy Slim, queue round the corner here for their Christmas turkeys.

'Further along the road, near where C & A is now, there was a store called Staffords; quite a fascinating place where they sold ornaments and fancy goods, the sort not seen at any other shops. In the afternoons they held tea dances. There was a small charge for a cup of tea, sandwich and cake. You could either sit and watch or participate in the fox-trot, waltz and the quick-step. The music was provided by a piano and a violin.'
Marjory Batchelor – A Life Behind Bars (QueenSpark Books, 1999)

Canhams © JJ Waller

Local Bookshops

British Bookshops and Stationers
www.britishbookshops.co.uk
This local company was formerly known as Sussex Stationers. Starting in 1971 as a family retailer, they have expanded across the south-east, and you're unlikely to walk down a main road in Brighton & Hove without coming across a store. Their main business is discount books - with a good number of local publications including a selection of QueenSpark's books - and a wide range of calendars, cards, pens and art materials. Check the website for store locations and telephone numbers.

City Books, 23 Western Road, Hove
(01273) 725306
'A ray of light in a corporate world!'
– Local resident
For over twenty years owners Paul and Inge Sweetman have tantalised our literary tastebuds with all that is current and exciting in the book market. City Books is a cornucopia of words - Inge always dreamed of owning a shop and the fact it's a labour of love is evident. Not only does the shop host its own high profile events at The Old Market round the corner, they also act as booksellers to most of the city's literary events including Brighton Festival.

Kemp Town Books, 91 St George's Road, Brighton (01273) 682110
www.kemptownbookshop.co.uk
Tucked away in Kemp Town is the city's other literary gem: Kemp Town Books.

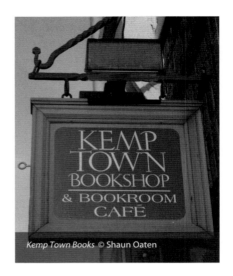
Kemp Town Books © Shaun Oaten

Owner Darion Goodwin has completed an extensive refurbishment over the last few years and the shop now boasts one of the best coffee shops in town and a converted cellar full of yet more books! There is always a warm welcome from Darion and his sidekick Megan (the shop's resident spaniel) and occasional events are held in the upstairs coffee shop where you can browse the sliding bookcases whilst sipping your cappuccino.

Second Hand Books

Unfortunately, Brighton and Hove isn't quite the second-hand book treasure trove it once was. However, it still probably has more second-hand books on offer than most British cities. From these establishments, you can quickly and cheaply assemble a personal library

Most second hand bookshops can be found in the Lanes

for any shelf that needs filling. A big part of the fun is scouring shelves and rooting through boxes, never knowing what you'll come home with. Here's our pick of some of the city's favourites….

Books for Amnesty, 15 Sydney Street, Brighton (01273) 688983
This charity shop has a dedicated bunch of volunteers who organise events like book swaps. Well worth a look.

Brighton Books, 18 Kensington Gardens, Brighton (01273) 693845
For identification purposes, this bookshop is often referred to as 'the one with the cat'. It does indeed have a very friendly cat, but that isn't its main draw. It is an aesthetically pleasing shop and has an impressive range of fiction and non-fiction titles including a good selection of paperbacks in boxes outside.

Two Way Books © David Gray www.imagesbrighton.com

Colin Page Antiquarian Books,
36 Duke Street, Brighton (01273) 325954
This is a serious second-hand bookshop
with a large general stock including
antiquarian illustrated & plate books.
*..always has a good selection of cheap
paperbacks outside. – Jonathan*

The Heart Foundation Bookshop,
76 London Road, Brighton
(01273) 674613
With books starting from 50p and great
promotions, here you can save money
and help the BHF. Volunteers are always
needed, contact the shop direct.

Invisible Books (At Snoopers Paradise),
7- 8 Kensington Gardens, Brighton
(01273) 602558
*This is probably my favourite. It's a small
but interesting selection and I always find
something I want to read there. – Tessa*

Oxfam Bookshop (Two shops)
30 Kensington Gardens, Brighton
(01273) 698093, 47 Blatchington Road,
Hove (01273) 733163

*Brighton is full of many second-hand book
shops, musty dusty places with hidden
gems. As a student, the Oxfam bookshops
are brilliant; they have nearly all the books
that are on the syllabus and many more.
– Loretta*

Rainbow Books, 28 Trafalgar Street,
Brighton (01273) 605101
Crammed full of books, they stock fiction
and non-fiction titles.

Sandpiper Books, 34 Kensington
Gardens, Brighton (01273) 605422
This quality remainder bookshop stocks
a lot of non-fiction hardbacks; American
University Presses, illustrated art and
architecture, Taschen etc. There is a £1
back room which is worth a visit.

Two Way Books, 54 Gardner Street,
Brighton (01273) 687729
Still hanging on to its slightly unkempt
1980s look, Two Way stocks an interesting
mix of books. Mainly dealing in paperback
fiction, you're just as likely to find a dusty
bodice ripper as a pile of old comics.

Music

© David Gray

You can't walk down the street in Brighton & Hove without bumping into a busker or a teen with a guitar. Music is a big part of life here, and the city is home to a number of top-class instrument and record shops. Whether you're after that first album by an obscure British psychedelic combo, an early Fender Strat or a CD by the latest Japanese thrash-punk girl band, you should be able to find it somewhere.

One Saturday afternoon, brother Teddy and I walked all over Brighton looking for a gramophone record of 'Yes, we have no bananas'. In the end we found one in Edward's music shop in London Road. We must have saved a long time to buy it because a ten-inch record cost one and threepence (6.5p) in those days.
Everything Seems Smaller – Sid Manville (QueenSpark Books, 1989)

The Acoustic Music Company, 39 St. James's Street (01273) 671841
These specialists in all things acoustic stock a wonderful array of guitars and there's always expert knowledge on hand.

Across The Tracks, 110 Gloucester Road (01273) 677906
Slightly chaotic (adds to the charm), you'll need to get on your knees to search through the boxes in this shop. You're bound to find something that you didn't know existed, and at a reasonable price. The boxes in the doorway are often worth a look too.

Borderline, 41 Gardner Street, (01273) 671447
Recently refurbished, the rather ramshackle has been replaced by clean lines and shelves, opening out onto the street. Whereas some record shops are cluttered and somewhat daunting for the less nerdy record searcher, Borderline has gone the other way. Vive la difference!

The Drum Cavern, 66 North Rd (01273) 665414
Guitar, Amp and Keyboard Centre, 79-80 North Road (01273) 672977.
Once only a tiny shop, the Guitar Amp and Keyboard Centre has expanded to two shopfronts and a drum shop up the road; this is testament to its comprehensive stock of instruments and very informed and friendly staff. They sell mainly new equipment, with some second-hand, and have a fair selection of tuition books too.

Fine Records, 32 George St, Hove
(01273) 723345
The name of the shop indicates that it
doesn't sell any of that popular
nonsense, but it does buy and sell a
wide range of classical and jazz CDs,
records and cassettes, and has a nice
little sideline in birdsong recordings.

Music Room, 90 Western Road, Brighton
(01273) 775607
Part of a national chain, but doesn't feel
like it. A wide range of guitars and
keyboards – with occasional diversions
into percussion and tin whistle territory
– are only dwarfed by racks of tuition
and chord books. The friendly staff and
the instructional DVDs playing on the
big screen make this a definite
destination for the beginner as well as
the accomplished player.

The Record Album, 8 Terminus Road,
Brighton (01273) 323853
www.therecordalbum.com
Famous within music and theatre circles,
much has been written about this shop
(check the folder full of press clippings).
Although The Record Album sells all
types of music in vinyl format, it focuses
on film soundtracks, stage, musicals and
high quality classical recordings. It also
stocks all genres of music on LP &
45rpm. All of the stock is either new,
unplayed or absolute mint, unless
otherwise stated. Owner George Ginn
reckons he has 15-20,000 vinyls, from
classical to pop, and they're in fantastic
condition. George has been in this
business since 1942, and in his present
location on Terminus Road, on the

Rounder Records © David Gray www.imagesbrighton.com

western side of the station, since 1962.
'I said it was too small', confides George,
'but my wife said "Take it". She had a
good feeling about it.' The location has
served them well so her instincts were
correct. Catch George in a quiet moment
and he might even play you some of his
favourite vinyls. The shop's speciality is
film, theatre and TV, and George has
links with the entertainment industry,
whose luminaries regularly use him
when they need a high-quality
recording. Famous customers have
included Simon Callow, Patrick Macnee

to host the occasional in-store gig and sell tickets for others. The stock is not the biggest – only CDs, and obscurities are not their forte – but it's bang up-to-date, and their 'Change from a fiver' section is well worth a browse.

Rounder Records, Brighton Square, Brighton (01273) 325440
For over 35 years Rounder has been dealing in vinyl (they apparently have eight tons of it) and now CDs. Their longevity is doubtless a result of the staff's knowledge and enthusiasm for old artists as well as new. With Fatboy Slim and Damian Harris as ex-employees, and voted one of the Top Ten stores by The Independent, they look set for another 35. Their Album Club (£10.00 a month and a staff-chosen album is delivered to your door), the bargain shelves filled with rare goodies and tickets for the hottest gigs in town make Rounder a top destination for music lovers.

Wax Factor, 24 Trafalgar St, Brighton
Rock-ola, 29 Tidy St, Brighton
both (01273) 673744
What a treat! Spend an hour browsing the immense and eclectic racks of books, CDs, vinyl, videos and other ephemera that fill the window and two floors of this Trafalgar Street store, then walk through the 'Rock and Roll Alley' door at the end of the Singles rack, into the café - a 1950's-themed joy that serves big coffees, adequate breakfasts and home-cooked lunches. Make a selection on the free 50's jukebox, then head back into Wax Factor for another hour…

of The Avengers, members of the Dad's Army cast and the author James Herbert. The Record Album has worked with the English National Opera, the Chicago Opera, with DJs and music producers, and was voted the Best Specialist in the country by The Independent.

Resident Records, 28 Kensington Gardens, Brighton (01273) 606312
Funky and fresh – the newest kid on the block – the knowledgeable staff are enthusiastic enough to promote their personal favourites, as well as find time

Snooper's Paradise © JJ Waller

Collectables

If you're into collectables, which covers just about everything from tin toys to vintage postcards, you'll find a host of shops in Brighton to satisfy your appetite. We've selected a few city stalwarts that have traded here for many years.

Coastal Stamp Auctions, 36 Queens Road, Brighton (01273) 324827
Coastal Stamp Auctions is a Mecca for collectors. Situated on busy Queens Road, it stocks old stamps, vintage postcards, cigarette packets and ephemera. There are certainly bargains to be had, but as presentation isn't their strong point, you may be there for a while searching for them.

Rin Tin Tin, 34 North Road, Brighton (01273) 672424
Stockists of old advertising materials and 20th Century collectables, including old advert labels posters, vintage magazines, signs and books, Rin Tin Tin is a wonderfully nostalgic place to spend time. Whether it's the purchase of that elusive gift for the person who has everything or the hunting down of a treasured film poster, this is the place to do it.

Snooper's Paradise (Flea Market), 7-8 Kensington Gardens, Brighton (01273) 602558
If you're in a hurry – forget Snoopers. You need plenty of time to browse the multitude of stalls selling anything from vintage postcards to a 70s Kaftan.

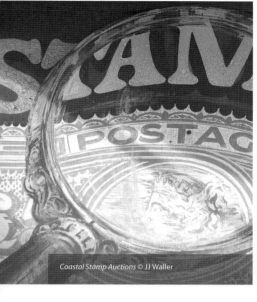

Coastal Stamp Auctions © JJ Waller

Yesterday's toys at Snooper's Paradise © JJ Waller

Step Back in Time, 125 Queens Road, Brighton (01273) 731883
Brightonian Robert Jeeves has been a collector since he was 18. Under his father's tutelage he began with stamps, but quickly moved on to postcards and this is the passion he has followed for the past 32 years. When you enter Step Back in Time, the shop Robert runs with his wife Tracey, you can see it belongs to a serious collector. They have been at their present location since 2001 and in addition to stocking a wealth of postcards from all over the world, they hold thousands of old photographs of Brighton & Hove and the surrounding Sussex towns and villages. The family run business also offers different services for its customers like framing old prints of Brighton or transferring prints on to canvas. You don't have to be a collector to enjoy this shop - it so unashamedly celebrates the city's past you cannot help but fall under the spell of these wonderfully evocative photographs and postcards. But be warned, you'll need to set aside a bit of time because you won't want to leave!

Valelink Ltd, 26 Queens Road, Brighton (01273) 202906
Just down the road from Coastal Stamp Auctions sits another gathering place for enthusiasts. Valelink Ltd has been at its present location for 26 years. John Trory and his wife originally opened it as a model railway shop but through the years they have diversified and it's now Brighton's leading seller of collectables. They continue to sell model railways but also stock old dinky toys, coins, banknotes, toy soldiers, old cigarette cards and even sell miniature replicas of Jones' van from Dad's Army.

Charity Shops

If your thing is picking up bargains that other people didn't know were bargains, then you're all set for a happy couple of days trawling the charity shops of Brighton & Hove. Head for the North Laine, St. James's Street, Western Road, London Road (Brighton) and Blatchington Road and George Street (Hove) where all the 'major' charities are represented.

The Martlets Hospice Shops

150 North Street/ 2 Church Street/ 97 Blatchington Road, Hove (01273) 730606/ 690132/ 747297 respectively. Furniture Warehouse at 270 Old Shoreham Road (01273) 721188 www.themartlets.org.uk
Local charity the Martlets Hospice in Hove has a number of stores around town that support its medical and nursing care for adults with terminal and life limiting illnesses. The charity also offers financial help, counselling and bereavement support to the families and friends of people in its care. Needing to raise more than £7000 a day to keep going is a tall order, and one well worth supporting. They sell good quality second-hand and nearly new furniture, kitchen items, paintings, small electrical items, silverware and ornaments, as well as evening wear, dinner suits and jewellery.

Emmaus, Drove Road, Portslade (01273) 426470
If you're interested in shopping for the second-hand and occasionally bizarre (or even if you're not, as it's worth seeing) get on the No.1 bus to Portslade Village and follow the prominent signs to Emmaus. The largest second-hand superstore in the south of England, it is a self-supporting residential community helping homeless people to help themselves, 'giving people a bed and a reason to get out of it'. They collect second-hand goods and sell them via their cavernous shops, situated in two parts of the site. From furniture to books, wine goblets to TVs, and literally everything in between, you should find something you want – and if you don't there is no better place to just browse. They also stock a large selection of plants & shrubs grown in the nursery garden. Between the two shops is a delightful café offering lunches, sandwiches and drinks.

Smoking

As Brighton & Hove has always liked to see itself at the forefront of radical action and personal liberty, some hoped that there might be room found in the city for those who like to share their 'vice' with others and in public. However, the lack of loopholes in the law has almost (see Burkitts, below) put paid to that. Still, the dedicated smoker can console themselves with the fact that there are a number of fine establishments in the city catering exclusively for them – and the rest of us can celebrate the fact that individual shops like this still exist.

Burkitts © JJ Waller

The Bead Shop © James Pike www.jimpix.com

Dockerills © David Gray www.imagesbrighton.com

Smoker's Heaven, 10 Queens Road, Brighton

Offers a huge variety of tobacco, cigars, pipes, lighters, paper, bongs, and accessories from around the world. It is not the most atmospheric of shops, but it's centrally situated, and open daily until 10pm.

Taylor's, 19 Bond Street, Brighton (01273) 606110

A humidified cigar room, a sign saying 'Thank you for Smoking' and a collection of quality loose-leaf tobacco tell you that this is a serious smoker's hangout. Big, big cigars, high-quality pipes, and a service for connoisseurs

Burkitts, 117 Church Road, Hove (01273) 731351

Opened in 1873 around the same time as the Metropole Hotel, this veritable institution has remained in family hands since then. Grade II listed, history wafts through the place, and is also on display in the many old photographs dotted around. Mrs Shelton, if prompted, may find time to tell you some tales, such as that of the WWII soldier who had found himself on Brighton beach after being evacuated from Dunkirk. In need of a smoke, he walked barefoot to the shop upon learning that they sold individual cigarettes! Due to a specially-granted license, the 'No Smoking' Health Act will not fully apply here, as smokers will still be able to light up one of their huge range of cigars and pipes (but not cigarettes) in the name of 'trying it out'. They also sell hand-crafted walking sticks.

Ivy's in the punk era © David Gray www.imagesbrighton.com

Shops That Defy Categorisation

These are traders who've been with us for years and deserve a mention.

The Bead Shop, 21 Sydney Street, Brighton (01273) 675077
www.beadsunlimited.co.uk
...a time machine. Go in. Browse. Come out and an unbelievable amount of time has passed. – Local resident
The Brighton Bead Shop has been open for 21 years. Owner Geoff Ellis recalls that their first day of trading was an icy March Saturday in 1986 when three inches of snow fell and they had taken £50 by the close of business.
This shop should adopt the slogan *'Truly Brighton'*, for where else would you find

such a quirky outfit? Geoff is an economics graduate who's used his financial nous to establish a slick enterprise that belies its unassuming 'I'm just-a-little-bead-shop-don't-hurt-me' name. The Bead Shop sells all manner of beads in all shapes, sizes and materials. There is glass, shell, enamel, leather, wood, plastic, steel, bronze and more. Some products come from far-reaching corners of the globe and The Bead Shop makes an effort to visit those suppliers and ensure fair trade wherever possible, which fits in with the eco-friendly spirit of the North Laine. The Bead Shop is also online. Orders are dispatched from the well organised Hove warehouse, usually same day, and a glance at the online comment book reveals that the customers, both national and global, are a hutchful of happy bunnies. Old documents show that The Bead Shop was probably the Abingdon Arms pub in a former life. Geoff says when it first opened, The Bead Shop stood out, surrounded as it was by glaziers, butchers, fishmongers and greengrocers. Nowadays, of course, the street's a whole lot trendier;

One afternoon a gentleman decided our shop doorway was more comfortable than his own bed. He proved impossible to move and was directly blocking the entrance. I was surprised to find that the customers took all in their stride and simply stepped over him. When an ambulance man eventually succeeded in helping him to his feet we discovered he had obviously forgotten to secure his belt and was last seen stumbling into Sydney Street with his trousers around his ankles. The North Laine has a well earned reputation for eccentricity - dull it ain't.
– Geoff Ellis owner of The Bead Shop

Dockerills, 3b Church St, Brighton (01273) 607434
Much more than just a hardware store, Dockerills is a Brighton institution. The family run business was started over 90 years ago by Walter Dockerill. The staff are friendly, helpful and knowledgeable. If it's a tin of paint you want or just a key cut - this place is central and convenient.

Ivy's, 33-34 Church Street, Brighton (01273) 328587
This outdoor shop selling vintage clothes is another Brighton institution and if the day came when it closed, it would be a sad loss to Church Street. It's not a shop in the conventional sense.

Most shops display their wares inside. Here, however, the clothes for sale are hung outside the shop, on the wall. Given that much of the stuff has a dramatic or striking quality, the effect is very arty. Michael Brown was born in Church Street and the *Ivy* of the shop's name refers to his mother. He has lived here since the Thirties; as such, he's well qualified to be able to offer up a tale or two about the changes that have taken place in the area. Ivy's specialises in evening wear, top hats, bowler hats, military gear, kilts and Scottish uniform, gentlemen's suits and coats. On the day we wandered up there was a greatcoat dating back to 1951 which was in pristine condition, hardly worn. The handwritten label showed J. Boot and the date it was bought, March 1951. There was also a professor's gown - handy if you suddenly come over all clever or feel the sudden need to dress up. Definitely worth a visit! You could come away with something you can guarantee no-one else will be wearing, or just have an interesting conversation. One can be bought, the other you won't find in any chain store…

North Laine Ceramics – Workshop Pottery, 94 Trafalgar St, Brighton (01273) 601641
www.workshop-pottery.co.uk
Located on Trafalgar Street, home to many valiant, independent and thriving businesses, this pottery studio opened in 1979 and, like many of the unique businesses in Brighton, has proved its staying power. The years have not been without incident though; in 1996 a

Bus in a china shop: North Laine Ceramics, hit by a bus in 1996 © Peter Stocker

hippy bus drove through the front window of the shop, which took four months to rebuild! The owner's Raku pottery reintroduced by popular demand is for sale in the shop. These pots are made by firing the clay in a propane kiln and once red hot, plunging them into wet leaves and shredded paper. The pots' resulting colours vary from copper red to blue lustres. The Pottery runs six-week courses for approximately £100, corporate events and school Clay Days. Check the website for relevant times and details.

Masquerade, 40 Preston Road, Brighton (01273) 673381/699944
Tucked away near The Duke of York's cinema, Masquerade (fancy dress and theatre costume hirers) has been

© Peter Stocker of North Laine Ceramics

operating for 18 years. Not bad for a place that 'seemed a good idea at the time' according to the owners. As well as being very busy at obvious times of the year (Halloween, New Year etc.), the shop is a major port of call for local colourful characters appearing in shows and pantomimes. The owner describes how the shop regularly sees boys in drag alongside gorillas and superheroes at the counter. Never a dull moment!

Ransoms, 2- 4 Ann Street, Brighton (01273) 686941
Something of the old timer on the block, Ransoms has been open for over 30 years selling domestic hardware and much more. Some of the older customers can remember when they would be sent by their parents to buy cockles and whelks from a lady with a donkey and cart outside this building.

Masquerede © J Waller

Nowadays, the donkey might be harder to come by but if it's a sink plunger or a quiche tin you want, this is the place. It's crammed full of essentials to satisfy all your domestic needs.

Namrick Ltd, 124 Portland Rd, Hove (01273) 736963
www.namrick.co.uk
Namricks was opened 25 years ago because the owner had difficulty finding nuts and bolts for his 1936 MG sports car, which is now fully restored. Situated in Hove on Portland Road the shop sells every conceivable kind of nut, bolt, screw or washer, and it has a mail order service which runs from the website.

The Ironing Shop, 74 Western Road, Hove (01273) 734893
Ironing as an artform! Whilst the concept of ironing might seem a bit passé, even the most slovenly student might need to present neat bib-and-tucker at a job interview. Here's the solution. At the top of Palmeira Square, near delis and boutiques, sits this totally incongruous dry cleaning shop. The front window displays two women assiduously getting the creases out and, while it's rude to stare, it's also very difficult to take your eyes off them.

Oliver's Clock Shop, 15 Cross Street, Hove (01273) 736542
Grandfather clocks, alarm clocks, antique clocks, novelty clocks, bits of clocks. It's a clock shop, and one which eschews all things digital in a wondrous two floors of tick-tockery. One wonders how it survives in a residential street and not

Open Market © David Gray www.imagesbrighton.com

even a sign above the door, but it does, and should (maybe the linked eBay shop is doing particularly well). Well worth a visit, even if just to peer in the window.

C&H Weston, 12 East Street
(01273) 326388
If smoking is frowned upon, then guns, knives, slingshots and other items with which to kill and maim are way beyond the pale; however, the well-informed staff in this shop sell to a discerning hunting clientele – although that doesn't quite explain the Gatling Gun in the front window – and cater for enthusiasts with a number of antique items. If you want to go the whole hog, you can also pick up a Barbour jacket amongst a range of hunting clothing. They have a lovely dog too.

Markets

Open Market, Marshall's Row
(between Ditchling Road and London Road), Brighton
www.openmarket.org.uk
The Open Market started life in 1919 as an unofficial market in nearby Oxford Street. In 1926 a permanent site was found on the gardens of Marshall's Row (the present site) following a sustained campaign by Brighton barrow boys (itinerant traders) who needed a permanent pitch to sell their wares. Opened in its present form by the Duke of Norfolk on 7th January 1960, it comprises of local traders selling all kinds of foodstuffs and goods, and is badly in need of an update. An £11

Upper Gardner Steet on market day © The Argus

million makeover is due to happen as part of a regeneration project. Hopefully the involvement of longstanding traders and stall holders will allay any local concerns that the redevelopment might lose some of the market's original character.

Sunday Market, Brighton Station Car Park (off Trafalgar Street)
This venue is home to serious traders as well as casual car boot sellers. Whilst the opening times are given as 9am-2pm, you may need to get there much earlier to get the real bargains.

Pre- the Open Market, **Upper Gardner Street** was the place where you would find the barrow boys (see Open Market); the road has maintained its place as a trading area, despite the occasional resident's objection. During the week, the North Laine Antiques Market keeps the trader flag flying, but on Saturdays the street comes alive with a range of food, second hand books and household goods sellers.

Gardner Street market in the 1940s © The Argus

Farmer's Markets

On the increase across the city, these markets cut out the middlemen and offer local produce direct to shoppers, responding to community concerns about food miles and demand for organic produce. Brighton & Hove Food Partnership and Common Cause Cooperative have linked with the Council to develop George Street Market in Hove (01273 470900) on the fourth Saturday of every month, from 10am-3pm.

Brighton & Hove Farmers Market is completely vegetarian, and operates from 10-3pm on the first Sunday of every month at Ralli Hall near Hove Station (01273) 323200.

The Farmer's and Fairtrade market – offering food and crafts - is held on the third Saturday of the month, from 11am-4pm at the Friends Meeting House, Ship Street, Brighton (01273) 770258.

Brighton & Hove maps

Town Centre

Seven Dials

Kemp Town

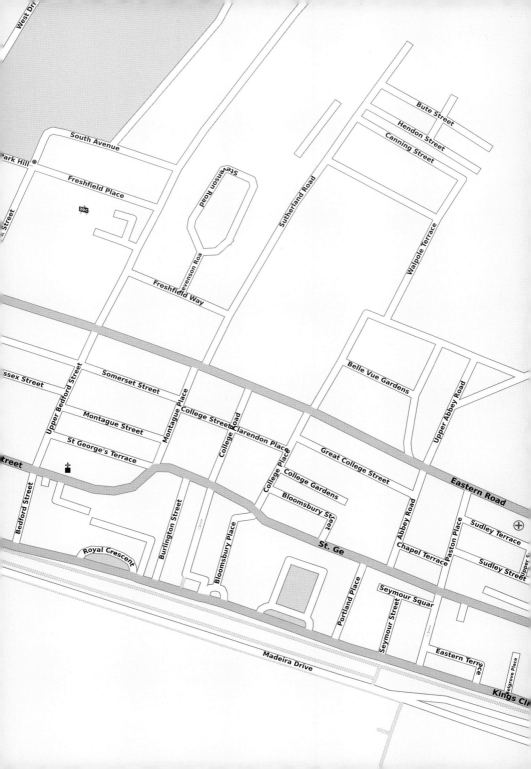

The Sea Front (part 1)

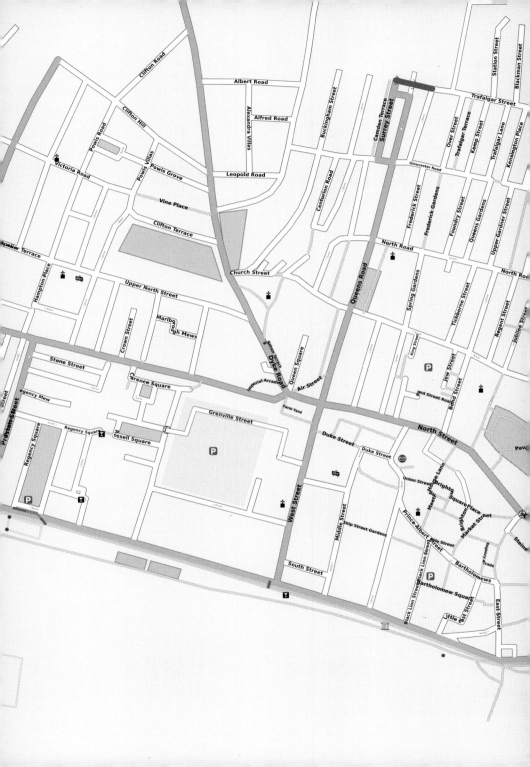

The Sea Front (part 2)

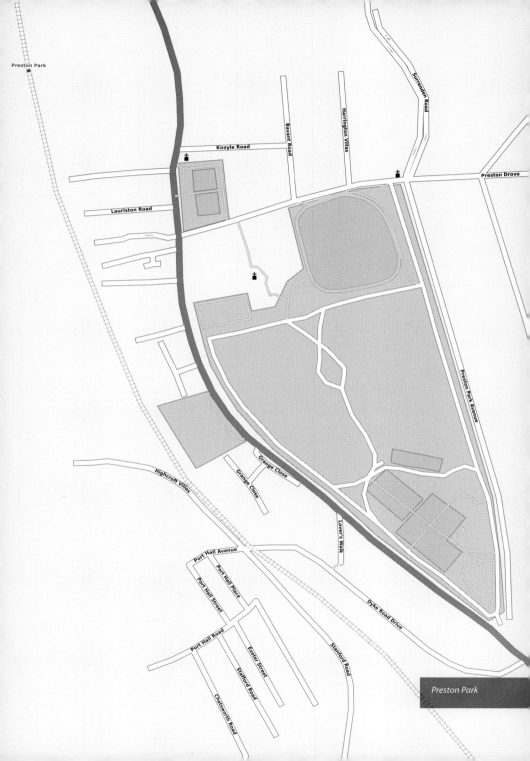

Preston Park

Hove

Hanover

Index

24 Hour Museum   98
Aberdeen Steak House   42
About Town   6
Acoustic Music Company   123
Across the Tracks   123
Active for Life   29
Al Fresco   38
Al Rouche   44
Anarchist Teapot   13
Ancient Mariner   71
Appendage   113
Archers   119
Argus Forum   29
Arkwrights   119
Audrey's Chocolates   116
Baby Boogie   17
Bali Brasserie   44
Bankers   44
Bar Valentino   82
Bardsley's   44
Barley Mow   69
Barry at the Tureen   48
Basement Arts Production   32
Basketmakers   77
BASS   17
Battle of Trafalgar   71
Bead Shop   131
Bedford Tavern   80
Best Cocktails   82
Best for Food   77
Best Pub Quizzes   81
Best Seasonal Pubs   70
Best Sunday Roasts   79
Bill's   58
Blackout   114
Blanch House   82
Blind Lemon Alley   45
Bodega D Tapa   46
Bombay Aloo   47
Books for Amnesty   121
Bookshops   120
Booth Museum   96

Borderline   123
Bothways   18
Bramptons   119
Bricycles   13
Bridge Community   32
Brighthelm Church & Community   31
Brighton Activist   29
Brighton Animal Action   13
Brighton Books   121
Brighton Coach Rally   87
Brighton Festival   88
Brighton Museum   96
Brighton Our Story   19
Brighton Pagoda   54
Brighton Rocks   79, 80
Brighton Tavern   80
Brighton Youth Centre   31
Bristol Bar   73
British Bookshops and Stationers   120
Browns Bar   82
Browns Bar and Restaurant   42
Buffet Island   43
Burkitts   130
Burning the Clocks   90
Bus City Sightseeing   6
Bus Company B&H   6
Bus Company Big Lemon   6
C&H Weston   135
Cabbies' Top Ten Restaurants   42
Cafes and Tea Rooms   58
Calendar of Events   87
Canhams   119
Caramella   116
Carden Park Community   31
Carluccio's   38
Casa Don Carlos   48
Charity Shops   128
Charles Street   80
Chattri Memorial Service   89
Cheaper Restaurants   44
Children's Parade   88
Chimney House   77

China China   42
China Garden   42
Chinese Centre   21
Christmas Swim   90
Circus Project   22
Cissy Mo   114
City Books   120
City Synergy   22
Clare Project   22
Coastal Stamp Auctions   126
Colin Page Antiquarian Books   122
Collectables   126
Colonnade   72
Community and Voluntary Forum   29
Community Base   32
Community Brighton   29
Community Mental Health   32
Community Noticeboards   12
Cornerstone Community   31
Cowley Club   32, 61
Crescent   81
Cricketers   67
Donatello's   43
Disability Advice Centre   31
Dockerills   132
Dorset   49
Druid's Head   67
Drum Cavern   123
Due South   37
Dumb Waiter   62
E. Sussex Community Info   29
Eagle   72
Earth and Stars   74
Earthship Project   14
East Brighton Bygones   24
E-Kagen   47
Emmaus   128
Estia   49
Evening Star   73
Expensive Restaurants   56
Extra Mural Cemetery   96
Fabrica   97

Farm   73
Farmer's Markets   136
Favourite Journeys/Walks   100
Fine Records   124
First Base Day Centre   32
Fishing Museum   93, 97
Fitzherbert Community   31
Food for Friends   50
Fortune of War   70
Fountainhead   81
Free Internet   98
Fresh Start Community   31
Friends Meeting House   31
Gallery Café   62
Gars   50
Gay Pubs   80
George   77
Gift Shops   113
Ginger Pig   78
Gingerman   39
Graffiti   97
Grand Parade of Authors   23
Great Eastern   73
Green Brighton   30
Green Women   14
Greys   78, 79, 81
Guided Walks   101
Guitar, Amp and Keyboard Centre   123
Hangleton Community   31
Hanover Community   31
Havana   56
Heart Foundation Bookshop   122
Heritage Open Days   98
Highlights   7
Hip-hop Festival   89
History Centre   19
Hollingdean Community   31
Homeless and Lonely   24
Hop Poles   78
Hotel du Vin   42
Hove   112
Hove Lawns   94

Hove Library   98
Hove Museum   97
Impact Initiatives   32
Indian Summer   56
Infinity Café   62
infinity Foods   116
Inside Out   62
Invisible Books   122
Irish Arts Network   29
Ironing Shop   134
Issues Forum   29
Ivy's   132
Jewish Centre   31
Join In   17
Jubilee Library   98
Kambi's   40, 47
Kaye Day Centre   32
Kemp Brasserie   51
Kemp Town   113
Kemp Town Crypt Community   31
Kemptown Books   120
King Alfred Leisure   31
King and I   51
King and Queen   69
Kings Road Arches   92
Kite Festival   89
Koba   82
La Capannina   51
La Gigo Gi   62
Lanes   112
Lavender Room   114
Lee Cottage   51
Legends   80
Lesbian and Gay Switchboard   32
Level   94
Lewes Crescent   106
Lewes Fireworks   90
Libraries   98
Linux User Group   30
Lion and Lobster   81
Lord Nelson   81
Louis' Beach Café   62

Mad Hatter   61
Magpie Recycling   14
Mai Ped Ped Ped   51
Marine Tavern   80
Market Diner   42
Markets   135
Marlborough   80
Marrocco's   62
Martlets Hospice Shop   128
Masquerade   133
Mayday in Albion   87
Meadowview Community   31
Mechanical Memories   98
Medium Priced Restaurants   48
Meeting Place   61
Migrant English   24
Mint   52
Mock Turtle   61
Momma Cherri's Big House   52
Mosaic   24
Moshi Moshi   41
Moulsecoomb Community   31
Moulsecoomb Wildlife   24
Mrs Fitzherberts   70
Muang Thai   52
Murasaki   52
Museums and Galleries   96
Music   123
Music Room   124
My Brighton and Hove   25, 30
Naked Bike Ride   89
Namrick Ltd   134
Neighbourhood Care   18
Neo   82
New Media   29
New Writing South   28
Nia   63
Nightwriters   28
North Laine   111
North Laine Photography   98
Nou Nou   54
Nurses Favourite Pubs   69

Off Beat 63
Office 71
Oldest Pub? 67
Oliver's Clock Shop 134
One Paston Place 43
Open House 79
Open Houses 88
Open Market 135
Oxfam Bookshop 122
Pablo's 47
Palace (Brighton) Pier 92
Parks and Gardens 94
Patcham Community 31
Pavilion Gardens 95
Pavilion Gardens Café 59
Peace Centre 13
Permanent Gallery 98
Phoenix Arts Association 32
Phoenix Community 31
Pintxo People 41, 82
Pioneer Motorcycle Run 87
Planet India 39
Polish Centre 32
Preston Park 95
Preston Park Community 31
Preston Park Tavern 78
Pride 89
Prince Regent Leisure 31
Prompt Corner 54
Pub Crawls 83
Pubs with a Story 73
Pussy 115
Queens Arms 80
Queen's Park 95
Queensbury Arms 68, 80
QueenSpark Books 28
Queer Mutiny 25
Radio Reverb 30
Rainbow Books 122
Ransoms 134
Rape and Crisis Centre 32
RareKind 28

Real Brighton 30
Real Eating Company 57
Real Patisserie 117
Record Album 124
Red Roaster 58
Red Snapper 47
Regency 55, 80
Regency Tavern 79
Resident Records 125
Resource Centre 32
Riddle and Finns 55
Rin Tin Tin 126
Robin Hood 75
Rock-ola 125
Rough Music 30
Rounder Records 125
Royal Pavilion Tavern 69
Sanctuary 58
Sandpiper Books 122
SchNEWS 30
Seafront 92
Seafront Office 92
Second Hand Books 120
Seven Dials 113
Sevendials Restaurant 57
Shopping Areas 111
Sidewinder 69
Smash EDO 17
Smoker's Heaven 130
Smoking 128
Snooper's Paradise 126
Somerset Day Centre 32
Southcoast Indymedia 30
Specialist Food Shops 116
Spectrum LGBT Forum 32
St Anne's Well Gardens 95
St Bartholomew's Church 96
St George's Inn 69
St Nicholas Church 95
St Patrick's Trust 32
Stanley Deason Leisure 31
Stanmer Park 95

Steamers   63
Step Back in Time   127
Streets of Brighton   88
Students' Union Brighton   30
Students' Union Sussex   30
Sudanese Coptic   25
Sunday Market   136
Sussex in the City   118
Sussex Playwrights   29
Sussex Square   105
Taj   118
Tallula's Tea Rooms   63
Taxis   6
Taylor's   130
Terre a Terre   37, 42
The Blue Man   46
The South   29
Threshold Women's Mental Health   32
Toast   61
Top Free Activities   86
Top Ten Buildings   8
Top Ten Pubs   66
Top Ten Restaurants   37
Top Ten Shops   110
Tower House Day Centre   32
Tubas Friendship   17
Tuc Tuc   6
TUC Unemployed Centre   31
Two Way Books   122
Upper Gardner Street Market   136
Valelink Ltd   127
Valley Social Centre   32
Velvet   115
Veteran Car Run   90
Wagamama   41
Wai Kika Moo Kau   61
Walks   99
Walmer Castle   81
Waterstone's   12
Wax Factor   125
Web Communities   29
West Hill Hall   31

West Pier   93
Whitehawk Community Food   26
Whitehawk Youth and Community   31
Withdean Leisure   31
Women's Centre   19
Women's Refuge Project   32
Woodingdean Community   31
Working for Change   13
Workshop Pottery   132
Worst Things   9
Writing Organisations   28
Yeoman   79
Young People's Centre   31
Yum Yum   118